THE LAND OF THE LONG LONG NAME

North West Wales Companion

John Lasarus Williams

Cyflwynedig i chwarelwyr Gogledd Cymru a'u gwragedd

Dedicated to the quarrymen of North Wales and their wives

Front cover sponsored by Virgin Trains
Credits Gwynedd County Council
First published 1999

ISBN: 0 9525267 19

Typesetting: Information Services UWB

Printed in Wales by O Jones (Printers) Llangefni, Ynys Môn / Anglesey

CONTENTS

Siân Owens with Section A Friars 'Dreams of Glory' one of many supreme champions bred by R Owens, Bryn Coch, Star, Gaerwen, Anglesey one of a few top breeders in North West Wales Telephone 01248 714687. (Welsh Pony and Cob Society, Aberystwyth 01970 617501.)

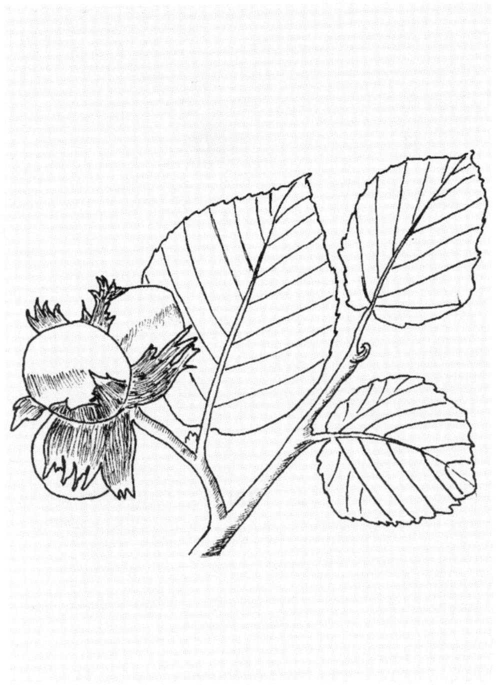

Hazel for luck

Patriotic postcard

ACKNOWLEDGEMENTS

There are so many friends who have helped me in the preparation of this book that I am unable to name them all. A number were named in my previous local history of Llanfair Pwllgwyngyll in Welsh but there are many others. I wish to thank them all most sincerely.

The members of staff of the libraries of the Local Authorities and those of the University of Wales, Bangor have been very helpful. I wish to record my particular appreciation of the help given to me by the Llangefni library staff and those at the Normal site.

My friends, Mr Glyndwr Thomas, Councillor Ieuan Llywelyn Jones, Mr Clive James and Dr William Griffith have kindly taken the trouble to read the whole of the typescript and have made valuable suggestions most of which have been incorporated. My wife has been at hand throughout to provide valuable assistance in the preparation of the type-written text. We are most grateful for the ready technical help given by Mr Vivian Allan Jones. During the final stages the technical and practical assistance given by Mr Dai Rees Jones and Mr Dafydd Roberts has been invaluable.

Co-operation in the form of grants from the Isle of Anglesey County Council and the former Gwynedd County Council was crucial in the encouragement it provided. Similarly, the support in the form of sponsorship of pictures by companies and organisations was a vital stimulant on a long and lonely project. I wish to thank the following most sincerely:

The Garden Centre, Holland Arms
The Snowdon Mountain Railway
Midland Bank, Menai Bridge Branch
Dr Haydn Edwards, Coleg Menai
Farmers Union of Wales
University of Wales, Bangor
The Environment Agency
The Transport and General Workers Union
Great Lakes Chemical
First Hydro
Anglesey Steam Rally
Railtrack
Llandudno Town Council
Eastman (Peboc)
Hogan Brothers
Dŵr Cymru
Ty'n Lôn Garage
Menter Môn
Virgin trains

For permission to reproduce pictures and illustrations I also thank the persons and institutions listed overleaf. Every effort has been made to find out the ownership of copyright. If in error a picture has been published without permission I wish to apologize. Finally I wish to thank O Jones, Llangefni for printing and producing an attractive book.

John L Williams
Llanfair Pwllgwyngyll

ILLUSTRATIONS
BLACK AND WHITE

COLOUR

INTRODUCTION

LLANFAIRPWLLGWYNGYLLGOGERYCHWYRNDROBWLL-LLANDYSILIOGOGOGOCH

It is surprising how many people in different parts of the world have heard about the very long place-name ending in *gogogoch* and found it amusing. These last three syllables could well be mistaken to represent the sound of a cockerel crowing, in Welsh, at the dawn of another day. Many thousands of people will have read about the long name, known to CB radio enthusiasts as Alphabet City, or received a postcard including the fifty eight letter name or even paid a quick visit and had their photo taken underneath it. And yet, when one mentions Anglesey, Gwynedd and Wales in distant countries only a few people have a vague concept of our country never mind our special part of it. This book is an attempt to remedy this situation.

A translation of the long name into English is given with an explanation of how it was made up and, for the first time, an answer to a hundred year old mystery, the actual name and identity of the person responsible. Part of the book is an adaptation of the author's Welsh language history of the village Llanfair Pwllgwyngyll and its environs.

Starting from this point of interest and taking Llanfair Pwllgwyngyll, close to Bangor, as a fairly central location with regard to North West Wales, the following pages seek to provide information about significant towns and places between Llandudno and Bardsey Island and between Holyhead and Aberdyfi. The area is highly significant in the history of Wales being the kingdom and the fortress of the royal line of Gwynedd. It is hoped that the book will provide interesting reading material and serve as a fairly permanent supplement to the excellent brochures produced annually by the County and Town Councils, particularly Anglesey and recently 'Snowdonia' by the Gwynedd and Conwy County Councils. In conjunction with adding to the enjoyment of visitors from other parts of Wales and from other countries, the aim is to foster in local residents, who do not normally read the brochures about their own area, a greater knowledge, a deeper understanding and appreciation of the spectacular landscape and the many attractions that are available on our doorstep. For our neighbours in Wrexham and the North East of Wales it is only an hour's drive by car along the A55 while it only takes four to five hours from South Wales. It is an appropriate time for us to destroy the myth of a great divide between South and North Wales.

Wales is not merely a region of England or of Britain. It is the home of the Welsh nation and in Welsh is called 'Cymru', the land of the compatriots. Professor Bedwyr

Lewis Jones wrote: 'The names *Welsh* for the people, *Wales* for the country go back to an Old English word which the earliest English settlers used to describe the Celtic speaking inhabitants of Britain. The same word can be seen today in the *wal-* part of place-names such as Saffron Walden (the valley of Welshmen), Walton (the village of Welshmen) and in the second part of the name Cornwall. Originally the word meant a foreigner. To the first Saxons the native inhabitants were foreigners; they spoke an alien language'.

This is how one Welsh historian, A H Williams described the Welsh. 'We are a people of mixed blood, living in a particular country and we have done so for centuries, speaking a particular language and that language the medium of expression of our religion, literature and music; and because we have lived together for many centuries we have our own history and distinguishing traditions. And that history and those traditions have in turn reinforced our nationality'.

A large number of people living in Wales do not speak Welsh. Many of them are Welsh and the parents or grandparents of many of them were fluent in the language. Whether they live in Gwent or Glamorgan or Clwyd or parts of Powys, the language of the area was Welsh until comparatively recent times. In this respect there is without doubt a Welsh cultural identity.

From an international point of view our nationality is conveyed most dramatically through sport with the help of television. The national anthem *Hen Wlad fy Nhadau* (Land of my Fathers), always sung in Welsh, and the flag, a red dragon on a background of green and white and the red jersey or vest are all powerful symbols. The soul of the nation is expressed poignantly in choral and hymn singing by large congregations. Through the English language aspects of our nationality have been recently portrayed memorably by Dylan Thomas, R S Thomas, Jan Morris, Emyr Humphreys and others.

Unfortunately there is a tendency to confuse nationality with race. We are not a particular race. Like others in Europe we are a mixed nation and there is little difference of blood between the Welsh and the English. Perhaps there is more of the Mediterranean temperament in our genes and more of the Nordic in the English. It has been said that we are much the same mixture, like plum pudding and Christmas cake.

TWO MOUNTAINS IN THEIR PLACE WILL ALWAYS REMAIN,
TWO PEOPLE, BY CHANCE, MAY MEET AGAIN.

WELSH PROVERB

WHERE ON EARTH?

For persons in distant parts of the UK and indeed of the world, who are curious about the place with the long name, Llanfairpwllgwyngyllgogerychwyrndrobwll-llandysiliogogogoch, the easiest way to locate it in the mind is to find a map of Britain and look for Anglesey (Ynys Môn) on the north coast of Wales. There are two impressive bridges over the Menai Straits connecting the island to the mainland, the Menai Suspension Bridge near Bangor and the Llanfair (Britannia) Bridge which is a railway crossing with a road deck above it. The centre of the village with the fifty eight letter name is within 1 mile (1.5km) of the Anglesey end of this bridge.

Some trains stop at Llanfair Pwllgwyngyll station. Alternatively, it is very convenient to take a small fast train from Chester or Crewe or the Intercity Holyhead train from London Euston to Bangor and get a bus or taxi from outside the station for the remaining 4 miles (6.5km). The same applies, in reverse, for travellers from Ireland through Holyhead. There is a train service between Bangor and Manchester Airport changing once at Chester or Crewe. The A55 is a dual carriageway road from Chester bringing road transport to within 1 mile (1.5km) of the village centre. This road along the North Wales coast, signposted to Holyhead, should be followed to the Llanfair (Britannia) Bridge. Near the entrance there is a large white on brown tourist attraction sign including Llanfair Pwllgwyngyll with the international *i* sign. On the Anglesey end Llanfair Pwllgwyngyll is again signposted in white on green indicating a slip road to the left off the by-pass. From here, passing the tall tower, the Marquess of Anglesey's Column, on the right, it is about 1 mile (1.5km) to the centre.

Here, adjacent to each other, are the Tourist Information Centre and the James Pringle shop. This tourist office with its brochures, videos and a welcoming atmosphere is a vital key to the understanding of Anglesey and North Wales; a short time spent here will be well rewarded. The addresses are as follows:

Tourist Information Centre
Llanfair Pwllgwyngyll
Station Site
Anglesey
LL61 5UJ
Telephone: (01248) 713177

Tourist Information Centre
77 Conwy Road
Colwyn Bay
LL29 7LN
Telephone: (01492)531731
Fax: (01492) 530059
E Mail: e:croeso@nwt.co.uk
Internet: http://www.nwt.co.uk

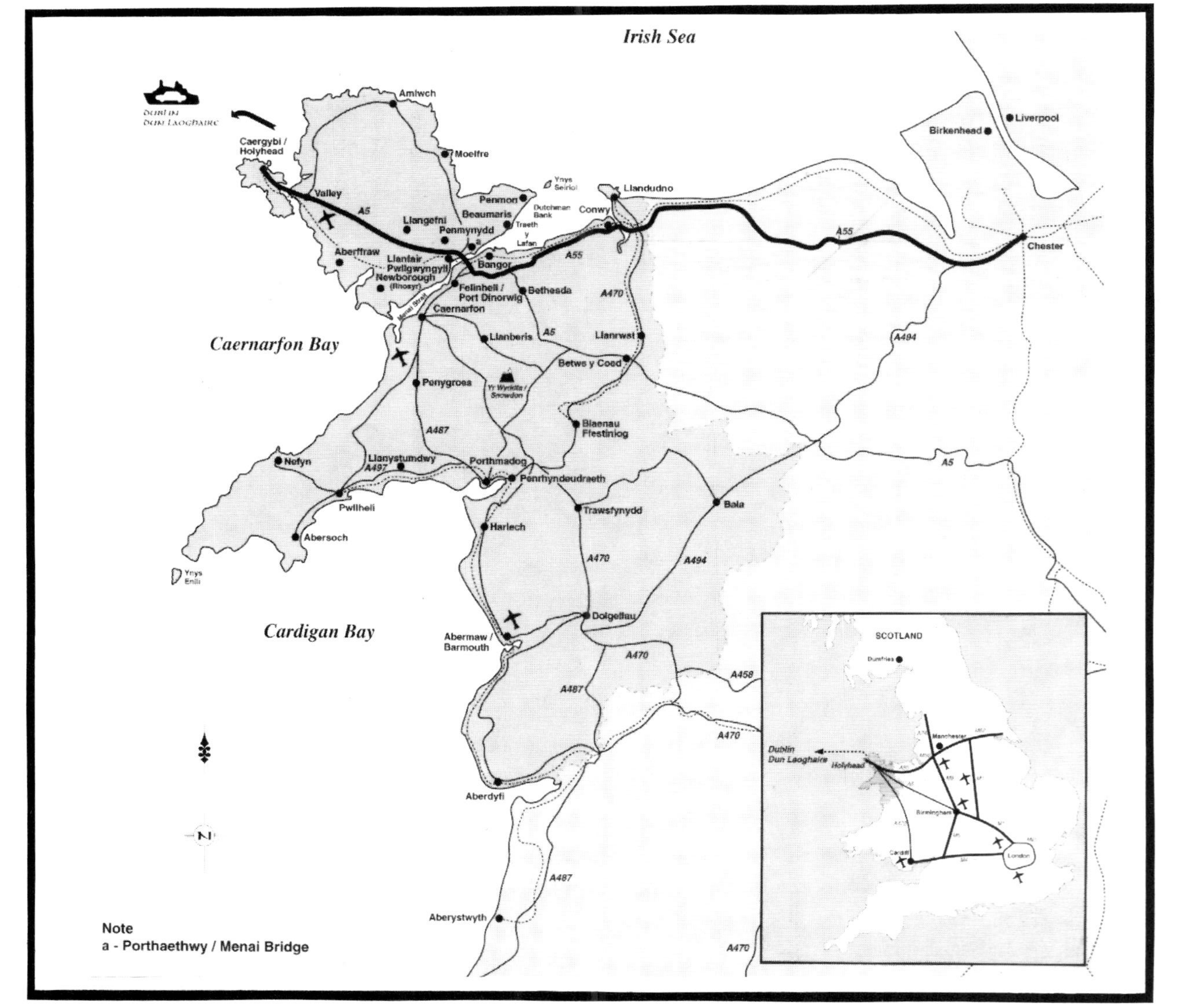

Map of North West Wales

Gwynne Owen

Around the centre there are plenty of opportunities to take photographs of the long name while some visitors will be lucky to hear village children saying it with no hesitation. Most people will enjoy a visit to the James Pringle shop and restaurant and read on a signpost the names of cities all over the world and the distances to them: Los Angeles 5235m; Buenos Aires 6879m; Berlin 752m; Tokyo 5923m; Inverness 295m. For a village this is a spectacular shop concentrating on woollens and clothing but including gifts made in Wales while the decor, incorporating the railway of the Victorian and Edwardian era, is fascinating. Compact discs of the world famous opera singer, Bryn Terfel and the outstanding boy soprano Aled Jones are usually available. Aled is from Llandegfan near Llanfair and Bryn Terfel was brought up on a farm at Pant Glas not far from Porthmadog. There are other interesting shops nearby and some restaurants and pubs serving meals. The chance of a chat with some of the bilingual residents will be an added bonus.

The Marquess's Column, a short drive in the car or a ten minutes' walk from the centre, provides panoramic views of the Straits and bridges, the mountains from the Great Orme to Yr Eifl in the west and overland as far as Holyhead. Many of these places are featured in this book. From Llanfair it is an important logical step to Oriel Môn near Llangefni, the market town and administrative centre of Anglesey. This is a modern interpretation centre and gallery which will create the proper mood to appreciate the history and mystery of the dark island, the last home of the Druids. In an article in the magazine *North Wales Lifestyle* published by *North Wales Weekly News*, Winter 1988, Christopher Proudlove recalls the circumstances leading up to the establishment of the permanent exhibition of the artist **Charles Tunnicliffe's** work. A collection of several hundred drawings and other works were to be sold at Christie's. At the last minute Anglesey Borough Council was able to secure the whole collection for £400,000 with the co-operation of The Royal Society for the Protection of Birds and The National Museum of Wales. Tunnicliffe was brought up on a small farm in Langley near Macclesfield in Cheshire and showed a remarkable ability to draw animals and birds from an early age. He was used to hard manual work at home but his talent was fostered in formal education including The Royal College of Art. He spent the last thirty two years of his life at Malltraeth in Anglesey studying and drawing wildlife. He was sought after as a book illustrator and commercial artist, one commission being wood engravings for *Tarka the Otter* by Henry Williamson. He produced his best work in Anglesey.

This and the numerous tourist attractions are magical little worlds that provide an educational experience as well as enjoyment. These are: Anglesey Model Village, Newborough; Anglesey Sea Zoo, Brynsiencyn; Foel Farm Park, Brynsiencyn; Tal y Foel Riding Centre, Dwyran; Anglesey Model Village and Gardens, Newborough; Parc Henblas, Bodorgan; Holland Arms Garden Centre; Bird World, Dwyran; Pili

Palas, the fascinating world of butterflies near Menai Bridge, and Stone Science near Pentraeth, all in Anglesey. Brochures about these attractions are available at the Tourist Information Centre, Llanfair Pwllgwyngyll. Also available are brochures about other attractions in the area covered in this book including the Greenwood Centre above Y Felinheli; Sygun Copper mine, Beddgelert; Brynkir Woollen Mill near Porthmadog; Rhiw Goch Ski and Mountain Bike Centre, Bronaber; Maes Artro Village near Barmouth; King Arthur's Labyrinth, on the A487 at Corris Craft Centre between Dolgellau and Machynlleth; and just outside, in Machynlleth, Celtica, the modern centre telling the story of the Celts.

Llanfair Pwllgwyngyll, on the Menai Straits, was formerly about a mile (1.6km) from the Porthaethwy ferry and in a central position with regard to the ancient courts of the Princes of Gwynedd at Aberffraw, Rhosyr, Llanfaes and Abergwyngregyn. Taking into account convenience of access it is quite central with regard to North West Wales. Today it takes about one hour to Holyhead and Amlwch by bus and through Bangor about the same time to Llandudno. From Bangor to Caernarfon should take about twenty minutes and from Caernarfon to Porthmadog about one hour. The furthest point is Aberdyfi, approximately a two hour journey by car.

There is another wonderful world within easy reach, our sister Celtic country, the land of magical landscapes, the land of literature, song and dance, the Emerald Isle and the city of Dublin (Baile Atha Cliath), with its Irish pubs and music; above all the Irish people, their history, their friendliness and their wonderful gift of talking. Within two hours from Holyhead one can stand in front of the site of the Easter Rising of 1916, the most famous Post Office in the world and read on Charles Stewart Parnell's monument the words: 'No man has a right to fix the boundary of the march of a nation; no man has a right to say to his country - thus far shalt thou go and no further'. Nearer the centre of O'Connell Street stands the Larkin monument with the inscription: 'They seem great because we are on our knees. Let us arise'. It is the land of the patriots including Patrick Pearse and Michael Collins and the great English language writers of the 20th century, George Bernard Shaw, James Joyce, J M Synge, Sean O'Casey and W B Yeats.

But we must be practical. The visitor, having studied the lists of accommodation, can decide where to stay early in the day, book through the Information Centre, and enjoy the rest of the day assured of a comfortable place to stay the night.

ROADS AND TRANSPORT

THE ROAD TO THE IRISH FERRY AT HOLYHEAD

The connection between England and Ireland or between London and Dublin was to a large extent responsible for the development of the village of Llanfair Pwllgwyngyll in the 19th century. The distance from Llanfair Pwllgwyngyll to London is 260 miles (418km) and to Caerdydd (Cardiff) 240 miles (386km). So the nearest capital city is neither of these but Dublin about 80 miles (128km) away. However the connection with Liverpool has been most important in two respects. Many people from Merseyside have been coming for holidays and day visits to the area for a hundred years and large numbers of men and women from North West Wales have moved to Birkenhead and Liverpool to find work. There they brought up families and formed Welsh speaking communities around the chapels.

OLD ROADS AND FERRIES

The Romans were excellent road builders. Their roads centred on London and one of them was called Watling Street, roughly the A5, from London to Viroconium, now Wroxeter, outside Shrewsbury with a connection to Deva or Chester. In Gwynedd they built a good road from Caerhun (Canovium) in the Conwy Valley to Segontium, their fort in Caernarfon and south to Tomen y Mur near Trawsfynydd. The Roman roads were the only good important roads until the 19th century.

In Anglesey the old roads which were very poor led to the ferries across the Straits. From the Middle Ages the most important ferry across the Menai Straits was that at Porthaethwy in the parish of Tysilio. In this name, *porth* comes from the Latin *portus* (port or ferry) and the second part refers to the local Celtic tribe, the Daethwy. In the 19th century the English name of the town became Menai Bridge probably because the railway station which was in Caernarfonshire had that name. For centuries the custom was for most of the cattle to swim across driven by men in boats. It has been claimed that 10,000 head of cattle were exported in 1794. People, horses and vehicles, sheep, pigs and other produce were carried over in ferry boats. From the Middle Ages there were as many as eight ferries across the Straits - Abermenai, Tal y Foel, Moel y Don, Porthaethwy, Porthesgob, Garth, Beaumaris and Llanfaes. By the early 19th century only five were operating, Llanfaes, Beaumaris and, it seems, Porthesgob having ceased to do so. Charles Harper in *The Holyhead Road* provides an insight into the working of the **Menai Bridge** or **Bangor ferry** with an inn on each side; the old George on the Arfon side which was extended in 1850, and where Swift the author of *Gulliver's Travels* stayed in 1727, and the Cambria, formerly The Three Tuns on the Anglesey shore. He says

'Up out of Bangor drove the Mails, and many of the stage-coaches, post-chaises, and chariots to the ferry-house. Thence passengers and their luggage were ferried across to the opposite side in boats and lighters each manned by four ferrymen. Coaches and chaises were in waiting when they landed, to whisk them off to Mona and Holyhead'. Post-chaises were light four-wheeled carriages hired from stage to stage or drawn by horses so hired while a chariot was a type of privately owned post-chaise owned by the nobility; lighters were flat-bottomed boats, or barges. In 1808 the mail was carried by coach instead of on horseback although the stage-coach carrying passengers travelled to Holyhead earlier.

The Garth ferry remained a useful short cut to Bangor for Llandegfan and other parts of Anglesey after the opening of the Menai Bridge in 1826 as did those to Y Felinheli and Caernarfon. The **Moel y Don ferry** to Y Felinheli was older than that at Caernarfon and had been an important trade route able to carry horses and goods to and from the town for many years. The boats to Caernarfon could eventually carry horses but they were not allowed to on fair days because the carriage of farm goods was so important. In the series *Caernarfon's Yesterdays* T Meirion Hughes has told the fascinating story of the vital link with Caernarfon for the farmers and school children of South West Anglesey in *Stemar Bach Sir Fôn* and other much loved craft. Although the little ships and boats have now become memories recalled in local history books and the Seiont II museum established under the leadership of Frank Rhys Jones the harbour is still busy during the yachting season and the age-old method of salmon fishing with a long net from the shore is still carried on. One of the large anchors of HMS *Conway* was rescued and restored by the Seiont II Trust. Weighing five tons it is on the forecourt of the museum by the Victoria Dock in Caernarfon.

THE DROVERS' WAYS

From the site of the old George Hotel, later the Normal College, half way between the Suspension Bridge and Bangor, the herds used to be driven over the Penchwintan part of Bangor, up Nant Ffrancon towards Capel Curig and Llanrwst a place to which animals from the Conwy valley, also, would come. From the Caernarfon hinterland they would aim for Pentir and Nant Ffrancon while the herds from Llŷn would be driven along the western side of Traeth Mawr, then over Pont Aberglaslyn on their way through Trawsfynydd to Ysbyty Ifan and Rhuthun. The cattle were also driven from Ardudwy to Trawsfynydd. At the end of a long journey to the Home Counties necessitating the cattle to be shod, they would be sold to be fattened for selling in London. It was a very important source of income for rural Wales.

LONDON TO HOLYHEAD VIA CHESTER
(CONWY, TRAETH LAFAN, BEAUMARIS, HOLYHEAD)

Since the reign of Elizabeth I the road to Holyhead had been one of the most important highways in the kingdom, Holyhead being designated as a posting station for the Royal Mail to Ireland in 1599. At that time the Royal Mail was carried on horseback from Chester, using a relay system of riders and horses changing at 'posts' or inns and crossing by the dangerous ferry over the River Conwy. Aber was the starting point for the shortest route across the sands to the Beaumaris ferry, then to the port and from there through Pentraeth to Llangefni, Bodedern and Holyhead. Certainly, when the turnpike road became available, Aber was the usual starting point and had been so for those taking the inland route through Bwlch y Ddeufaen. At low tide this was fairly convenient as there were some guide posts fixed in the sand, but it was dangerous and later, a warning bell was placed in the tower of Aber church for the benefit of those coming from Anglesey. Beaumaris Corporation had the guide poles renewed from time to time and spent money on the maintenance of the track using stones and faggots. The route from Conwy ferry was across Morfa Conwy along the sands below Penmaen-bach and Penmaen-mawr and across Traeth Lafan to the Beaumaris ferry, as is shown on John Ogilby's road map (1675). Before the turnpike road along the coast was built it seems that travellers would keep on the sands below Penmaen-bach without going to Aber. The anxious travellers would have to time their crossing carefully and it was advisable to employ the services of a guide who had tide tables. Some people crossed barefooted. There are pictures by J M W Turner (1775-1851) of a coach with large wheels, riders on horseback and people walking across the Lancaster Sands. The convenience of this method when roads were poor can be realized by walking or riding a horse on the sands at Red Wharf Bay in Llanddona. This must be done with great care without venturing far from the high water mark. The authoritative book on the topic of the ferries is *The Conway and the Menai Ferries* by H R Davies.

THE BEAUMARIS FERRY

The Beaumaris ferry was situated until 1690 where the Green is now and then moved to the Point. It is possible that the altered nature of the sandbanks was the reason for the change. The white building referred to as a landmark was probably the ferry house at the Point. In 1631 the boat was big enough to carry four horses, and being flat bottomed was therefore designed to float in shallow water. The prow and the stern were high and the sides very low so that people could wade into the water and step inside. While ferrymen inside the boat lifted the horses' forelegs, others up to their waist in water, would push and urge them on with a stick.

HORSES: DANGEROUS AT BOTH ENDS AND UNCOMFORTABLE IN THE MIDDLE

A record from 1562 reads: 'Richard White has been post of Bewmarys since 1561'. The opportunity to travel across the Lafan Sands extended to just three hours out of twelve and this was impossible during foggy and stormy weather. H R Davies points out that the post could not be delayed with the result that the 'post-boys' would often be forced to ride to Porthaethwy Ferry.

HORSES AND COACHES

There is an account of coaches and a wagon going over the sands and being ferried across the channel. It was 1686 and they belonged to Lord Bulkeley and Lord Clarendon. H R Davies concludes that this only happened on very rare occasions and employing some craft larger than the ferry, both on the Beaumaris and Conwy crossings. But the Conwy ferry must have been a fairly large craft because William Williams, Llandygai recorded that, in Cromwell's time, it sank with the loss of about eighty lives with only one young woman surviving. And there is a reference to a large boat capable of carrying carriages and horses at Beaumaris. H R Davies, quoting William Bulkeley, gives an example of the funeral of Mrs Meyrick in 1742 travelling from London to Anglesey, in which the hearse and the mourning coaches were ferried across the Straits at Porthaethwy and therefore over the Conwy as well. And he refers to a letter by William Morris of Holyhead in 1753 in which it is said that eight coaches, chariots and post-chaises had arrived at the Port travelling along the same route. However Davies maintains that, prior to the middle of the 18th century, few people travelled across North Wales other than on horseback. Moreover, during the 17th and early 18th centuries ordinary travellers would normally go to Bangor and cross at Porthaethwy where the crossing was narrow, available at all states of the tide and not liable to disruption because of bad weather. In 1721 Bangor was regarded as being on the great road from London to Holyhead. The small boats of Porthaethwy which could only carry three horses were supplemented by larger ones capable of carrying coaches. The embarking and disembarking points on both sides were near the position of the Suspension Bridge while Porth y Wrach, slightly to the east on the Anglesey side was also used.

THE MOUNTAIN ROUTE

At high tide and in rough weather it was possible to go round the back of Penmaen-bach through the Sychnant Pass along old pack-horse tracks and continue on similar paths on the high ground and behind Penmaen-mawr mountain to Llanfairfechan and along the coast road to Bangor and the Menai Straits ferry. Another option for travellers on foot or on horseback was to follow the track over the notorious obstruction of Penmaen-mawr. Some crossed the Conwy at Tal-y-cafn ferry and took the Roman road through Bwlch y Ddeufaen which was also a prehistoric route. Apart from the two upright stones, hut circles and burial chambers, nearby is the important hill-fort **Pen-y-gaer** commanding a view of the lowlands around comparable to that from a helicopter. This strongly walled fort on a hill rising to 1,247ft (388m) in the parish of Llanbedrycennin is of special interest because, apart from the usual very thick walls consisting of large blocks with rubble in the middle, the ramparts are guarded in the most vulnerable parts by two areas of pointed stones set close together on the slope to form what are called *chevaux de frise*. They would act as a barrier to men on foot or on horseback.

TROUBLE AHEAD

During the 17th and the beginning of the 18th centuries the roads even in England were atrocious, stretches of mud in places making it impossible for wheeled vehicles to progress so that goods were carried by pack-horses. For example, Charles Harper in *The Holyhead Road* mentions that goods between London and Shrewsbury were carried by pack-horses and that in 1737 a large heavy vehicle called the Gee-ho was introduced. It was drawn by eight horses and took just over a week to go to or from London. This did not, at once, replace the pack-horses. A later development, in 1750, was the *Shrewsbury Flying Stage Wagon* again carrying goods such as Welsh flannel and butter and which provided an opportunity for the less well-off to travel by coach.

One can therefore imagine the great danger of **Penmaen-mawr** and the fear it instilled in the traveller especially in rough weather. The road was a mere stony track on the side of the mountain with steep cliffs underneath and the real possibility of rocks falling from above. A dramatic, if alarming, entrance to Snowdonia. Towards the end of the 17th century a new road was built lower down and this was again improved at the beginning of the 18th century. In 1772-74 another attempt was made to improve matters by building a new road designed by Sylvester. During the 18th century the roads were steadily improved by the Turnpike companies while the coaches became less cumbersome, more comfortable, lighter and faster. The Sylvester road over Penmaen-mawr with a wall on the seaward side and some form of defence against landslides was a great improvement and the first coach traversed it in 1776. The Chester to Holyhead mail coach was able to use it in 1785.

LLANGEFNI AND LLANNERCH-Y-MEDD

After 1765 diversions and improvements were made to the road from Porthaethwy to Holyhead going through Llangefni and Bodedern, the old post road, with four tollgates, at Braint, Llangefni, Llanynghenedl and Caergybi (Holyhead). Beaumaris with its fine houses had been the main town of Anglesey but in 1785 as a result of the new road the small village of Llangefni became a market town and after 1800 the place developed rapidly. It has been the county town since the 1880's and is undergoing major changes again. The central and important Bob Parry Farmers' Mart has recently been closed and some buildings dismantled leaving a very large area available for development. The planning of this and the road system in the town is crucially important for the future. The new headquarters for the Isle of Anglesey County Council is being built close to the centre. Llangefni is fortunate in having Nant y Pandy, the Dingle, a wooded valley with a footpath running along the banks of the River Cefni from the church of St Cyngar and the River Cefni has the potential to become a very attractive feature of the town. Llannerch-y-medd on the other hand, which had a market from 1657 and was, during the 18th century the foremost commercial centre, began to decline. In the first part of the 19th century there were two hundred and fifty shoemakers working in Llannerch-y-medd. In 1867 the first workhouse in Anglesey was built there.

INTO THE HEART OF SNOWDONIA

After 1802 a new road was built from Capel Curig over Penygwryd to Llanberis or alternatively through Aberglaslyn and Tremadog. It was therefore becoming much more convenient for antiquarians, artists and tourists to venture into the heart of Snowdonia. A reminder of days gone by is the stage-coach parked opposite the Ty'n y Coed hotel at Capel Curig.

A NEW GATEWAY TO CAERNARFONSHIRE

Leaving the famous picturesque Aberglaslyn Pass and the bridge we go past Nanmor where during the 1950s the hillsides were transformed for filming *The Inn of the Sixth Happiness* with Ingrid Bergman taking the part of the brave missionary Gladys Aylward. It was the home of one of the best of the professional Welsh language poets of the 15th century, Dafydd Nanmor, and another older poet, Rhys Goch Eryri, who composed interesting disputatious poems. As we go down towards Tremadog it is difficult to imagine the low-lying land as a vast expanse of sand called Traeth Mawr with sometimes the incoming tide rushing in in huge waves forced by a south-westerly gale. That was the position before W A Madocks built the embankment in 1812, called the Cob, across the mouth of the estuary. Early in the 17th century Sir John Wynn of Gwydir had tried to initiate such a scheme unsuccessfully. The completion of the project, reclaiming a very large area of land, providing a road and a short cut between Caernarfonshire and Meirionethshire and making it possible to establish **Porthmadog** harbour in 1821, was a major achievement. He had gained confidence to tackle the project through previously reclaiming successfully a large area near his home of Tan yr Allt. For supervising the building of the embankment and Tremadog he depended heavily on his able clerk of works John Williams. The well-planned streets and the buildings of Tremadog serve as a lasting tribute to both men. The street names, London and Dublin, are reminders of the dream that there would be a coaching station here on the way to Porthdinllaen and the ferry to Dublin. They probably also influenced the development of Porthmadog with its straight wide main street. On the left hand side on the road from Tremadog to Porthmadog stands the birthplace of Lawrence of Arabia, now a Christian Mountain Centre.

It was appreciation of this engineering feat, the Cob at Porthmadog, that enabled a poet, the young Percy Bysshe Shelley, to persuade the leading landowners of Anglesey at a meeting in Beaumaris to undertake a similar far-reaching scheme at **Malltraeth** reclaiming the expansive Cors Ddygau and providing a good connection between Newborough and Malltraeth. It is an interesting point of design with respect to Porthmadog Cob that, being wise after the event, it was realized that building from both ends to meet in the middle was a mistake because in doing so the sea was constrained into a powerful inrush near the mouth of the river making it extremely difficult to close the final gap. With regard to Cob Malltraeth a great deal of work had been done in 1790 but in the winter of 1791 a storm caused a serious breach in the embankment. The work was completed in 1812.

LONDON TO HOLYHEAD VIA SHREWSBURY

The first challenge to the Chester to Holyhead route was a compromise. It was usual for coach enterprises to be run in conjunction with inns. Robert Lawrence, the landlord of the *Eagle and Bell* in Shrewsbury ran a coach service between Shrewsbury and London in partnership with Payton of Stratford upon Avon. Lawrence could see that a shorter, more direct route from London to Holyhead could bypass Chester and go through Shrewsbury which would be to his benefit and that of Shrewsbury. In 1779 Lawrence set up a coach service to Holyhead via Wrexham, Mold, St Asaph and Conwy. It ran three times a week, the journey taking one and a half days. In 1780 Lawrence started the first stage-coach service between London and Holyhead going through Coventry, Castle Bromwich, Birmingham, Walsall, Wolverhampton and Shrewsbury but continuing to go through Conwy. It was in 1801 that the parliaments of Dublin and London were united, thereby emphasizing the need for a good stage-coach road from London through Shrewsbury to Holyhead. In 1802, after persevering in his project for many years, Lawrence was able to take advantage of Lord Penrhyn's road improvements from Bangor to **Capel Curig** where Richard Pennant, Lord Penrhyn had built a large inn. With a fortune from sugar plantations in Jamaica at his disposal he set about the organization of the slate industry on a large scale with the help of William Williams, Llandygai, originally from Trefdraeth in Anglesey, and the estate agent Benjamin Wyatt who was responsible for the attractive designs of estate houses in the neighbourhood. They developed the quarry, its administration being in the safe hands of Williams, had a rail track laid down from the quarry and built the port at Aber Cegin, Bangor in 1790. The Ogwen Valley road which is still open goes along the western side of Dyffryn Ogwen to the Ogwen waterfalls while the part from Llyn Ogwen to Capel Curig was to the south west of the present road. In 1802 the Capel Curig Turnpike Company built a new road on the eastern side of the valley, and consequently Lawrence could send the coaches along the new route avoiding Conwy and Penmaen-mawr. In 1808 the General Post Office decided in favour of the new Holyhead route through Capel Curig and, working with the Government, improvements were carried out by Telford along the whole length of the road during the next few years. The stretch of road between Capel Curig and Llyn Ogwen was re-routed to its present path and a new bridge was built at the entrance to Betws-y-coed. The Waterloo Bridge was built of cast iron in 1815, having a single span, decorated with a rose, a thistle, a shamrock and a leek in the iron work. These developments were leading up to the crowning project, the building of the Menai Suspension Bridge.

COACHES

By 1825 because of road and coach improvements, long distance coaches achieved the amazing speed of a hundred miles a day. How the *Shrewsbury Wonder* was able to do this is explained by Charles Harper in *The Holyhead Road*: 'The stud of horses kept for the *Wonder* numbered one hundred and fifty, all sleek and plump. None of the horses worked more than one hour out of the twenty four, being required merely on one of the ten mile stages, which they frequently performed in five minutes under schedule time, and then were taken fresh and vigorous from the traces. They were fed liberally, with the view of keeping them heavy, rather than muscular; strength for short and powerful exertion being required, rather than endurance. Their average value was £20 and they were seldom worked for more than four years on this fast coach'.

Tolls to be taken at
LLANFAIR GATE.

s. d

For every Horse, Mule, or other Cattle drawing any Coach or other Carriage with springs the sum of ... 4

For every Horse, Mule or other Beast or Cattle drawing any Waggon, Cart, or other such Carriage not employed solely in carrying or going empty to fetch Lime for manure the sum of ... 3

For every Horse, Mule, or other Beast or Cattle, drawing any Waggon, Cart, or other such Carriage, employed solely in carrying or going empty to feteh Lime for manure the sum of ... 1½

For every Horse, Mule or Ass, laden or unladen.

Llanfair gate tolls *Photo Derec Owen*

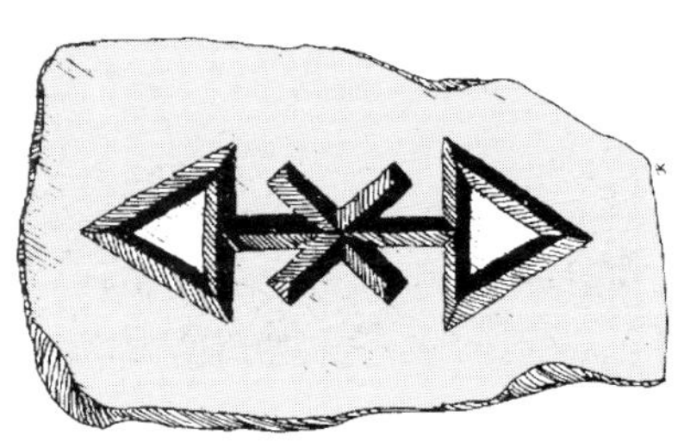

Telford's mason's mark

Llanfair Tollgate *Gwynedd Archives*

Chester to Bangor mailcoach from aquatint by Henry Alken
Courtesy John Cowell

Page sponsored by Hogan Brothers.

TELFORD'S ROADS

By 1830 Telford had completed his work on the A5 and also the road between Conwy and Bangor including the suspension bridge at Conwy (1826) and further improvements at Penmaen-mawr. The most significant fact about Telford's Holyhead Road is that despite the mountainous terrain the gradients are easy. In 1836 the Holyhead Mail covered the 260 miles (418km) in 26 hours 55 minutes. Between 1818 and 1822 the new road through Llanfair Pwllgwyngyll to Valley was constructed with five tollgates, Stanley, Caergeiliog, Gwalchmai, Nant, with the one in Llanfair being the last to be built. The Anglesey tollgates operated until November 1895 and they were the last in Britain. The coaching inn *Mona* and the embankment across the Stanley sands which took a few years longer to build, were part of the project. It was after the building of this road by Thomas Telford that Llanfair Pwllgwyngyll started to develop. The Welsh Office has recently designated the A5 from Llandygai to Chirk as a road of historical importance.

THOMAS TELFORD

Thomas Telford, the engineer responsible for building the Conwy and Menai Suspension Bridges was a Scotsman, the son of a shepherd from near Dumfries. Apprenticed as a stone mason, Thomas gained access to a private library and read widely. After some time in Edinburgh he obtained work in London and gained further building experience in Portsmouth docks and in Shrewsbury. His first bridge was at Montford near Shrewsbury. Not far away is one of his masterpieces, the aqueduct at Froncysyllte near Llangollen, 1,007ft (307m) long and carrying the Llangollen Canal opened in 1804 as a branch of the Shropshire Union Canal.

THE MENAI SUSPENSION BRIDGE

It was in spite of strong opposition by Caernarfon that the Menai Suspension Bridge was built in 1826. As late as 1818 MPs with other members of local gentry and tradesmen objected violently to the proposal. The Menai Straits had long been a stumbling block for improvements to the Irish road and serious consideration had been given to taking the mainland route to Porthdinllaen in Llŷn. However in 1776 a crossing near the site of the present bridge involving embankments from each shore and a bridge in the middle had been proposed and later a wooden viaduct with a drawbridge in the centre. The first plans were defeated by opposition from Caernarfon strongly supported by Assheton Smith and other influential local members of the ruling class. The main concerns were the important shipping interests and the prosperity of Caernarfon. Towards the end of the 18th century the Caernarfon Harbour Trust had been set up and had spent around £500 blasting rocks at the Swellies, the most dangerous part of the channel in the Straits near the

Original Menai Suspension Bridge

Bridge, Belgian Promenade and St Tudno 3 (1926-61)

Carpenter's workshop converted into bicycle shop Llanfair Pwllgwyngyll

William Jones's garage Llanfair Pwllgwyngyll. Where William Jones's bicycle shop used to be, by 1922 there was an impressive garage. William Jones had the trade plates 001 and 002. It is claimed that this is the first petrol pump in Anglesey. On the left the Ford Model T belonging to Lady Hughes Hunter, Plas Coch; centre a Morgan runabout and on the right a Singer. On the extreme right there is a bus that was used to carry children to Beaumaris Grammar School, registration EY448. The timber body was made in Bryn Salem workshop by Owen Hughes, Creigle and Tommy Lewis, Upper Village. John Griffith, Cae Cyd used to drive the bus. The figure standing by the motor bike is William Jones.

Photos Mrs Dilys Owen

Suspension Bridge.

The abutments with their majestic arches, three on the Arfon coast and four on the Anglesey side, and the massive supporting towers 153ft (47m) high were built of Penmon limestone. The tall-masted ships of the time made it necessary to have the bridge so high. The original sixteen iron chains (four sets of four) were hauled into position with capstans from a large raft across the Straits. Each chain weighed 121 tons and 290 pounds and they were anchored in tunnels into the rock at both ends. The length of the suspended parts of each chain between the two main piers forming a curvature was 590ft (180m). Not only was the bridge an outstanding engineering feat, it is a construction of great beauty. The original tolls were: foot passenger 1d, drove of cattle 1s 0d, horse, mule or ass 2d, horse-drawn carriages and coaches 2s-3s.

Between 1938 and 1941 the Suspension Bridge was partly reconstructed. The present four steel chains were the main improvement of the work undertaken by Dorman Long.

A few years earlier Caernarfonshire County Council, between 1930 and 1935 undertook a major improvement at Penmaen-mawr incorporating a tunnel through Penmaen-bach, two through Penmaen-mawr and a concrete and stone viaduct having seven arches.

Thomas Telford died in 1834 and was buried in Westminster Abbey. Robert Stephenson's grave is next to Telford's. Telford, the Shropshire new town, was named after the engineer.

CHESTER TO LLANFAIR PWLLGWYNGYLL: THE NEEDS OF THE NINETIES

The dualling of the A55 was undertaken by the Welsh Office in co-operation with Clwyd and Gwynedd County Councils. The 62 mile (100km) road improvement was a twenty five year project involving major engineering feats including the tunnel at Penmaen-bach opened in 1989 and the one at Pen y Clip opened in 1993 as well as the Conwy Tunnel, opened by Queen Elizabeth II in 1991. Sir Wyn Roberts MP, from Llansadwrn, Anglesey, as the Welsh Office Minister, was responsible during the crucial fifteen year period 1979-1994. Howard Humphreys were the specialist consultants for the two road tunnels built in 1934 and again for these recent improvements.

The consultants for Penmaen-bach were Travers Morgan and the contractors Balfour Beatty Construction. The whole section which cost £35,000,000 included the 722yds (660m) tunnel driven through the rock supplying a dual carriageway for westbound traffic while eastbound traffic goes along the old road. Laing Civil Engineering was the contractor for Pen y Clip or Penmaen-mawr and Travers Morgan the consultants. The cost of this stretch of road was £110,000,000 and includes a 0.6 mile (1.0km) hard rock tunnel for westbound traffic with the eastbound traffic using the improved headland road.

The most spectacular scheme, although unobtrusive now, is the Conwy crossing where Travers Morgan were again the consultants with Costain Tarmac as contractors. This crossing involves going under the River Conwy through Britain's first immersed tube road tunnel. The six reinforced concrete tubes were built in a prepared basin near the estuary. Each tube is 129yds (118m) long, 26.4yds (24.1m) wide, 11.4yds (10.4m) high and each weigh 33,000 tonnes. Temporary bulkheads fitted to the ends enabled the massive concrete tubes to be floated after the basin was flooded. They were lowered into position by charging the ballast tanks inside the tubes.

These three features are the most dramatic elements of an impressive project gaining many awards and including numerous other engineering feats. Detailed attention has been paid to environmental aspects. Special grass and wild flower seed-mixes were developed to blend into the natural surroundings and a large area of wetland has been created at the Conwy Estuary to form an attractive bird sanctuary near Llandudno Junction.

During the construction work the impact on water quality was closely monitored by the National River Authority, one of the predecessor organisations of the new Environment Agency. As mitigation for the envisaged impact on the fishery the Conwy Falls Fish Pass was constructed. The Environment Agency is currently evaluating the success of this imaginative project which has the objective of increasing the amount of spawning grounds available to salmon and sea trout in the Conwy valley. This scheme is unique in that the pass is in the form of a tunnel. A close watch is kept as the effect on the fish going up-stream could have international significance.

This link, the A55, is vital for the economic well-being of North West Wales. One of the most advanced industries in Gwynedd, the award winning EuroDPC at Glynrhonwy, world leaders in medical technology and molecular biology, would not have been located near the foot of Snowdon without this facility. It makes it possible for export goods to be on a plane in Manchester Airport within two hours. The road reaches Llanfair Pwllgwyngyll and there is an urgent need for it to be completed to Holyhead providing by-passes for the A5 villages on the island.

Realizing that air links will probably be important for development in the future, the Isle of Anglesey County Council's latest business estate is situated near the Mona airfield. By far the most important airfield in the area is RAF Valley, established in 1941, primarily a base for fighter training, but also used for helicopter sea and mountain rescue. It has also a meteorological station. With a view to civilian communication in the future the airfield at Llandwrog near Caernarfon is being improved. The new year, 1999, has brought very good economic news for North West Wales. The Dublin-based company Bimeda producing veterinary pharmaceutical products will soon be established at Bryn Cefni, the Llangefni industrial estate, providing initially, seventy high skill jobs. The company's UK head office will be at Llangefni. On the mainland the Slate Valley Initiative has received a grant of £3.2 million from the Welsh Office with matched funding of £3.4 million from Gwynedd County Council, the Welsh Development Agency, Celtec, local working groups and the tertiary colleges. It is hoped that this deprived area will soon qualify for Objective 1 Status i.e. it will be eligible for the highest level of European regional assistance.

AUTOMOBILE PALACE, LLANFAIR PWLLGWYNGYLL

William Jones's garage which used to be on the site of the Kwik Save store was taken over by Automobile Palace of Llandrindod. This was one of the largest garages in North Wales employing 128 workers around 1970. The facade of the old William Jones garage was similar to that of Ty'n Lôn garage.

Morris 8 Split Screen

Ty'n Lôn Garage, Llangefni is a Rover Dealer

Rover Ten 1935

Monfa Cafe, now Ty'n Lôn car park

Ty'n Lôn Garage c.1960 Aethwy RDC to left

Ty'n Lôn Garage 1984 with Volvo 245 Estate, 1979 T reg

Volvo started producing cars in Sweden in 1944; distributed UK early 1960's.

Page sponsored by Ty'n Lôn Garage

RAILWAYS AND RESORTS

There had been discussions during the first part of the 19th century whether the terminus of the new road from Shrewsbury should be Holyhead or the fishing port of Porthdinllaen near Nefyn in Caernarfonshire. In 1836 Llandudno was suggested as a terminus for the new railway to the Irish Ferry and in 1837 Porthdinllaen was being considered. Llandudno was soon rejected but it took five years for the matter to be resolved. It was only after a concerted campaign by leading Anglesey figures and the intervention of George Stephenson that it was decided, by just one vote, that the railway should end in Holyhead and not Porthdinllaen.

The original company, the Chester and Holyhead Railway, opened the railway from Chester to Bangor and from Llanfair to Holyhead in 1848 as recounted by J M Dunn in his detailed but concise book *The Chester and Holyhead Railway.* The building of the Tubular Bridge over the River Conwy provided Robert Stephenson and the other engineers with valuable experience when they faced the problem of building a bridge over the Menai Straits. The two tubes made of iron plates riveted together were constructed on the shore, floated on pontoons and lifted into position by means of hydraulic presses. Mr Evans was the name of the contractor. At Penmaen-mawr apart from the 231yd (211m) tunnel it was necessary to build a canopy to protect against avalanches and a viaduct to carry the track over the sea shore. Bangor station stands between the Bangor Tunnel, 913yds (835m) long and Belmont Tunnel 614yds (561m) long. On Anglesey the first station is Llanfair and after leaving the highest point between Llandudno Junction and Holyhead at Gaerwen the line goes over Malltraeth Marsh and the River Cefni on a nineteen arch viaduct. The next major construction was the widening of the Stanley Embankment to take the line to Holy Island and Holyhead.

In 1848 the engines operating on this line were called; Britannia, Menai, Bangor, Caernarvon, Flint and Chester. In 1856 the working of the railway was taken over by the London and North Western Railway. The famous *Irish Mail* first left Euston on the same day that the line was opened for public transport from Llanfair to Holyhead, i.e. 1 August 1848 but at that time that train had to stop at Bangor, the bridge crossing to Anglesey not having been erected, while another train completed the journey to Holyhead.

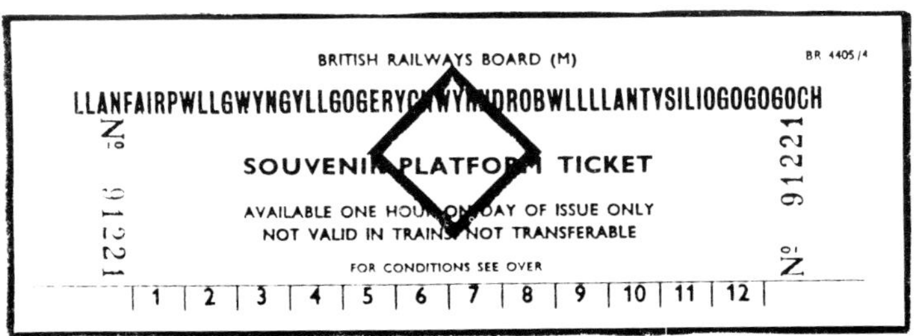

Menai Straits and bridges looking west before 1860. What is the clue?

Bridges looking east

Station long name in rustic wood painted white by W R Williams

THE RAILWAY STATION LLANFAIR PWLLGWYNGYLL

March 1848	The first train from Llanfair to Holyhead carrying officials only.
March 1850	The station was first opened.
March 1965	A hearing for objectors to the closure was held.
During 1965	Station closed.
April 1968	Some buildings demolished.
May 1973	Station reopened after closure

THE LLANFAIR BRIDGE (BRITANNIA)

The old tubular bridge was one of the great engineering feats of the 19th century. It consisted of two rectangular tubes of wrought iron, their shape like the outside of a matchbox, side by side, 25ft (7.6m) high by 15ft (4.6m) wide resting on massive stone pillars. The iron plates were 0.63ins (1.6cm) thick. The iron was brought to the site by sea as was the red sandstone from Runcorn for the inside of the pillars. The four limestone lions 25ft (7.6m) long and weighing 30 tons are the work of the sculptor John Thomas, of Welsh descent.

The bridge was designed by Robert Stephenson, the son of George Stephenson, the designer of the steam locomotive, the *Rocket* in 1826. The first train went over the bridge in 1850.

The huge blocks of dressed Penmon limestone used to build the three central pillars and the two abutments, one at each end, with their fine joints, deserve a close look to appreciate the craftsmanship. To bring these very heavy slabs of stone from the quarry on barges, to trim them by hand, and then to raise them with the help of timber scaffolding was in itself a remarkable feat. But the outstanding achievement was to get the four gigantic tubes into position and to do so in a part of the Straits where there are strong currents.

On land, at both ends, it was possible to construct the tubes in their final positions working from the timber scaffolds but four other sections were needed between the pillars across the water. They were built on wooden pontoons on the Arfon shore, the tubes being built by joining the iron strips with hot rivets. One tube measured 172ft (52.4m) in length and weighed 1,500 tons.

When the builders were ready, 20 June 1849, it was decided at an appropriate time according to the state of the tide and the wind-force, to release the two pontoons with the first tube resting on them to float towards the pillars. They were guided by tugs with ropes and cables from the shore where capstans were manned. The scheme was to guide one end towards the bottom of the Anglesey pillar and then

Construction of Tubular Bridge (1849) *Illustrated London News*

Floating of first tube *Gwynedd Archives*

to swing the other end into position at the base of the central tower. Having succeeded in that perilous task, the next step in the project was to raise the tube up 100ft (30.5m), a marvellous achievement. That was accomplished using hydraulic pumps, carefully packing underneath the ends every few inches and taking advantage of the valuable experience that building the Conwy bridge had provided. The three remaining tubes were floated to the pillars and raised in the same way.

In addition to all the workers, Mr Fairbairn, Mr Hodkinson and Mr Edwin Clarke, the engineer in charge, deserve credit and according to Robin Richards in *Two Bridges Over Menai*, also Mr Evans from Conwy who was able to persuade Stephenson that the best plan was to build the tubes on the shore and float them down. The principle of having two parallel tubes resting on stone pillars and sliding on brass ball bearings proved not only strong enough but also rigid and suitable for carrying heavy trains. The same principle can be seen in plant life in the comparative strength of a cane or even straw which are circular light tubes. The height of the bridge shows how tall were the masts of some of the sailing ships of the time. Finally, stringent tests involving three locomotives, wagons of coal and carriages of passengers were carried out to the satisfaction of Robert Stephenson.

The name *Britannia* is a misnomer taken from the name of the rock on which the central pillar rests. In a chart by Lewis Morris in 1748 the name is *Carreg* (rock) *Frydain* and the hypothesis is that *frydain* comes from the adjective *brwd* which has as one of its meanings, *effervescent, turbulent*, a most apt description of the sea breaking against the rock.

On the evening of 23 May 1970 the bridge was accidentally set on fire by boys looking for birds' nests. There was a strong breeze from the south west and once the fire had a hold on the timber and pitch of the roof there was no way of controlling the flames. It raged on throughout the night across the bridge from the Arfon side towards Anglesey, the intense heat causing the ironwork to sag. At about five next morning there was a very loud bang as though the complete structure had collapsed but what had really happened was that the fire had reached a paint shop inside the Anglesey pillar causing an explosion. It was impossible for trains to cross again until the steel arches that reinforce the present structure were in position. But vital beams for a crane required for building the aluminium plant at Holyhead were hauled slowly on a flat wagon attached by hawsers to winches at each end. The winches enabled the hawsers to be kept taut taking most of the weight off the damaged track.

Reconstruction started in 1972, Husband and Company being the engineers and Cleveland Engineers in charge of the building. The design incorporates a new road deck above the railway. It is necessary to restrict driving speed and stop access for high vehicles when there is a high wind.

In St Mary's churchyard nearby there is a memorial tombstone to the fifteen men who lost their lives during the building of the first bridge and the two during the reconstruction.

The building of the railway which was started in 1845, and the station, had a greater influence on Llanfair than the road. The railway bridge was completed in 1850. The age of steam had arrived but only horse-drawn vehicles would be on the roads for more than another half a century.

Where the centre of the village of **Llanfair Pwllgwyngyll** is today was then marshland dotted with cottages and smallholdings. A lake extended from the station site to Aber Braint and the fields to the south of the station are still subject to flooding. Building the road and the railway necessitated land drainage and much of the low-lying land that had been meadow and marsh became available for development. Houses, shops and a hotel began to appear. The station, the first on the island, was convenient for passengers from a large area and eventually it became a depot for coal and goods for the retail trade as well as a collecting point for livestock to be transported to England. Llanfair Pwllgwyngyll, towards the end of the 19th century, was a hive of activity. The thunder of the great wheels of the trains, the steam and the smoke, created an atmosphere of drama and adventure. The enchantment of distant places, formerly associated with the ships that sailed between North West Wales and the far-off ports of the world, was now a thrill to be experienced at a railway station.

The London and North Western Railway Company, was taken over in 1922 by the London, Midland and Scottish. Nationalization took place in 1948. The North Wales Coast main line is now the responsibility of *Railtrack*, which is investing heavily in the West Coast line from Euston to Glasgow and the North Wales County Councils feel confident that there will be substantial investment in the line from Crewe to Holyhead in the near future. With the Government's commitment to public transport and care for the environment the future looks promising.

The changes brought about by the development of railways after the 1840's were greater than the effect of building motorways over a century later. In 1848 when the station was opened in Bangor there were 5,000 miles (8045km) of rail in Great Britain. What had happened in the large industrial areas of coal and iron was reflected in the development of the great slate quarries of North Wales. The rail track for horse-drawn trucks to carry slates from the quarry at Bethesda to Porth Penrhyn in Bangor was laid down in 1800, the first rail-way in Caernarfonshire. A similar line was built from Dinorwig quarry to Y Felinheli in 1824 and from Dyffryn Nantlle to the harbour in Caernarfon in 1828. The first narrow gauge railway in the world to adopt locomotion was the connection between the quarries of Ffestiniog and Porthmadog, a port specifically built for exporting slate goods. In 1881 the population of Blaenau Ffestiniog was a remarkable 11,274. Gradually locomotives replaced horses on other lines to facilitate this extensive trade exporting slates to Ireland, France, Germany, Scandinavia, Australia and the United States. Work on the Ffestiniog Railway began in 1833 and was completed in 1836. Inclines to tackle some of the hills were replaced in 1840 when the Moelwyn tunnel was opened and from then on the trucks came down by gravity over easy gradients and they were pulled up by horses to the quarry. Steam locomotives were introduced in 1863 and in 1869 the first Fairlie locomotive called *Little Wonder* revolutionized the operation of narrow gauge lines. After many years of decline and neglect the Ffestiniog Railway was reopened in 1955 as a tourist attraction carrying passengers over the Cob for 13.5 miles (21.7km) through an isolated part of the Snowdonia National Park, an experience to treasure.

The London North Western Railway was in operation all along the North Wales coast by 1849. During the same year a development was taking place between the Great Orme and the Little Orme which was to become the resort of Llandudno with accommodation for 8,000 visitors by 1856. In 1852 a station was opened in Caernarfon and by 1867 the main line was extended to Afonwen, Pwllheli and Porthmadog.

BRANCH LINES

The next step was to open branch lines: Llanberis, 1862, Betws-y-coed, 1868, Nantlle, 1872, and Bethesda, 1884. There was a remarkable difference in Betws-y-coed in a few years. The first visitors, before there was a train, were mainly artists painting near Pont-y-pair and other picturesque spots. As the Rivers Llugwy and Lledr join the Conwy there are a number of bridges near Betws-y- coed. One famous artist was David Cox (1783-1859) the English watercolour painter who painted many romantic scenes in North Wales among the most famous being *Rhyl Sands* which is in the Victoria and Albert Museum in London. He was a regular visitor to Betws-y-coed from 1844. By the end of the 19th century there were a number of new buildings, hotels, boarding and lodging houses with a few shops and eating houses; there were guide books and photographs and excursionists taking snaps with their cameras. During the summer months many visitors would go, as they still do, to admire the Swallow Falls on the River Llugwy, the English name being the mistaken translation for the bird *wennol* instead of the correct *ewynnol* meaning foaming. At the Betws-y-coed Motor Museum there are normally over thirty motor vehicles on display. The interesting Conwy Valley Railway Museum is in the old goods yard of the station. The line from Llandudno through Llandudno Junction, Llanrwst and Betws-y-coed to Blaenau Ffestiniog is still open and has the longest railway tunnel in Wales measuring 2 miles 341yds (3.533 km).

Similar dramatic changes were seen along the North Wales coast following the sea bathing vogue in the early 19th century. The attraction of the beach and the sea brought hundreds to the Bangor and Caernarfon hotels and places by the sea developed into towns and resorts as at Penmaen-mawr, Llanfairfechan, Pwllheli and Criccieth.

From the 1920s as a result of competition from motor cars, buses and lorries the decline of the railways started. Passenger services were discontinued to Llanberis and Red Wharf Bay in the early 1930's and to Bethesda in 1951. But with the Beeching cuts of the 1960's communities in West Gwynedd were deprived of a valuable service while the tearing up of the railtrack was bureaucratic vandalism.

THE CAMBRIAN COAST RAILWAY

The Aberystwyth and Welch (sic) Coast Railway opened a length of track between Aberdyfi and Llwyngwril in 1863 and in 1867 the Cambrian Railways opened the route to Pwllheli, the bridge over the Mawddach estuary having been built in the same year. Again in 1867 the line from Bangor to Caernarfon was extended to Afonwen. Not only was it then possible to travel by train from Bangor to Pwllheli; one could go as far as Aberystwyth and South Wales.

Nearer our own time, in 1965, under British Rail, there was a train drawn by a steam locomotive from Pwllheli to Dovey Junction through Shrewsbury, Wolverhampton, Birmingham to Paddington. Leaving at 8.20am it arrived in Paddington at 4.00pm. Up until 1965 there was a train from Pwllheli to Swansea via Aberystwyth. In 1987 a service to and from Euston from Pwllheli was available in a train of several carriages drawn by a class 37 diesel loco.

The trains are now run by *Central Trains* and the important telephone number for information is 0345 484950. The single line is remarkable for the way it keeps very near the coast for most of the way. It provides a vital link between Porthmadog and Harlech crossing the timber bridge over the River Dwyryd between Penrhyndeudraeth and Llandecwyn. This bridge, Pont Briwet, also carries a toll road providing a short cut to Harlech thus avoiding many miles through Maentwrog.

Maentwrog, of course, deserves to be visited to appreciate the scenery of the Valley of Ffestiniog and to see the village. Archdeacon Edmwnd Prys (1544-1623) who composed metrical versions of the psalms in Welsh and helped Bishop William Morgan in the translation of the Bible lived at Tyddyn Du, Maentwrog from 1576 until his death in 1623. Another important literary figure was born at Cynfal not far away. He was the Puritan Morgan Llwyd (1619-59), best known for his classic prose work *Llyfr y Tri Aderyn* (The Book of the Three Birds).

PORTMEIRION

Not a lot needs to be said about 'the most magnificent folly in Britain', the Italianate village created by Clough Williams Ellis. The attractive buildings with sculpture-decorated gardens and the hotel by the sea have for many years attracted royalty, film stars and authors. It has become more widely known since the 1960's when the television series *The Prisoner* was filmed there. It is not far from Penrhyndeudraeth but it is better to leave the train at Minffordd and walk the remaining distance which takes about twenty minutes. The Cambrian Coast stops at both places. This masterpiece of recycling is a challenge to the throw-away society and an inspiration to careful people who reclaim old timber, stones and artefacts.

HARLECH

The particular attraction of the Cambrian Coast Railway is that it combines the enjoyment of the beautiful scenery with access to the popular resorts between Pwllheli, Barmouth and Aberdyfi. One of the highlights of the journey is a grand view of Harlech Castle from the train but it is better to have a meal and a look round the town and castle. The castle is different from the other three great Norman castles in Gwynedd in that it is high up above sea level. It is said that in the 13th century the sea reached the rocks underneath. But now there are extensive sand dunes where the railway and the station are situated. Also on the low-lying land is the Royal St David's Golf Club, in being since 1894 and the most famous of the numerous golf courses in Gwynedd. For some people it will not be the golf course that will bring back fond memories but the college for mature students called by some 'the second chance college' which has provided an opportunity for personal development or for many, an entrance to a career. The road, on fairly high ground, leading from Harlech towards Dyffryn Ardudwy provides one of the most stunning views even in Gwynedd. There are roads from Llanbedr inland and eastwards to good mountain-walking country towards Bronaber and Trawsfynydd or to Bwlch Drws Ardudwy between Rhinog Fawr and Rhinog Fach. The first goes along the banks of River Artro to Cwm Bychan at the end of which there is a path uphill called the Roman Steps but which is in reality a pack-horse track. On the other road to Nantcol stands the little chapel *Salem* made famous by Curnow Vosper's painting. Ellis Wynne (1670-1734), author of the classic prose work *Gweledigaetheu y Bardd Cwsg* (Visions of the Sleeping Bard), was born at Y Las Ynys near Harlech. From 1704 until his death he was the rector of several local parishes. His home, Y Las Ynys, has recently been restored.

Mochras or Shell Island near the village of Llanbedr is very popular for bathing and fishing. It is possible to drive a car along a causeway and after paying a fee enjoy a walk and a picnic.

A little to the north of Harlech lies the small church of Llanfihangel-y-traethau (St Michael's in the Estuary) and the churchyard where Jacqueline Kennedy attended the funeral of Lord Harlech.

BARMOUTH

The most spectacular part of the line is the 800yd (731.5m) long magnificent viaduct over the Mawddach estuary connecting Abermaw (Barmouth) to Y Friog (Fairbourne). Opened in 1867 it is the longest timber estuary bridge in the world. The channel of the river runs near the Barmouth end of the bridge, so it was necessary, to have originally a drawbridge and later a metal swing bridge to accommodate the ships that served the mines and quarries inland. The bridge was partly reconstructed in 1906 and 1909. During the 1980's there was great concern because the timber construction was being attacked by a marine worm. The future now looks brighter because Railtrack is investing heavily in the line and this important bridge. In 1883 and 1933 landslides caused fatal accidents at Y Friog making it necessary to build a concrete protective canopy over a part of the line while a few miles south between Tonfanau and Towyn, where the track follows the sea shore, huge boulders have been taken by rail to the vulnerable part to protect the line. There is another small timber trestle bridge over the River Dyfi.

The first property acquired by the National Trust was Dinas Oleu, or Oleddf a four acre rocky hill-top above Barmouth, the site of an Iron Age hill-fort. It was given by Mrs F Talbot, a friend of John Ruskin.

The sandy beach is today the main attraction of **Barmouth** or **Aber Maw** or Mawddach, the estuary of the River Maw, abbreviated in Welsh to Y Bermo like Y Berffro in Anglesey for Aberffraw, the definite article 'y' taking the place of the first 'A'. Barmouth harbour is attractive and boating and fishing facilities are available. Lewis Lloyd in *Sails on the Mawddach* points out that the port of Barmouth was more accurately the port of Barmouth-Dolgellau, Dolgellau being the centre of the Meirionnydd woollen industry. The port and fishing village was busy when small ships went to English ports and as far as Ireland, Spain and Italy exporting the coarse woollen cloth. Other important exports were timber and oak bark from the woodlands along the Mawddach. The river, navigable for some miles to Llanelltyd near Dolgellau, was important for small craft and there were quays and shipbuilding yards such as Llyn Penmaen (Penmaenpool), where a toll bridge was built in 1879. Not many years ago there was a tragedy in which many lives were lost when a pleasure boat sank at this spot.

Bont Ddu is interesting because of the **Clogau** gold mines in the hills behind it from which gold for royal wedding rings has been mined. Another goldmine, **Gwynfynydd**, lies north in Coed y Brenin near Ganllwyd. At one time around the turn of the century there were as many as 500 men involved in the industry in the Dolgellau area. Both have been working intermittently and they can be approached by public footpath. Copper, iron and lead ore were also exported while the imports to the merchants, shopkeepers and tradesmen included fish, salt, tea, coffee, sugar etc. The Mawddach remained important as a means of communication and commerce until the age of the train. The search for the goldmines may well lead to a very rewarding experience, the thrill of seeing the water tumbling down the waterfalls, Rhaeadr Mawddach and Pistyll Cain in silver cascades.

Some of the houses in Abermaw seem to cling to the rocky hillside and one interesting building is the Round House, a lock-up or gaol built early in the 18th century. The 19th century church in Abermaw is an attractive building and there is another interesting church, the parish church of Llanaber nearly 2 miles (3.2 km) from the town.

THE TAL-Y-LLYN RAILWAY

The Tal-y-llyn Railway from **Tywyn to Abergynolwyn** and extended to Nant Gwernol is Britain's first preserved railway. This 6.5 mile (10.5km) narrow gauge line used steam locomotives from the beginning in 1865 to carry slates from a quarry near Abergynolwyn and passengers to a point convenient for climbing Cadair Idris and visiting the fortress of Castell y Bere. The railway was almost derelict in 1950 but in that year the Tal-y Llyn Railway Preservation Society was established and restored it.

CADAIR IDRIS

Cadair Idris is a long mountain the highest point being 2,927ft (892m) overlooking the interesting town of Dolgellau. Its main features are the corrie basins carved out of the mountain side one of which has been captured in a typical golden-tinted landscape painting of Llyn Cau, which is in the Tate Gallery, by the influential Welsh painter Richard Wilson (1714-1782) born at Penegoes near Machynlleth and brought up in Mold. Before the popular Romantic appreciation of natural scenery towards the end of the 18th century Wilson had painted Cadair Idris and Gainsborough had painted scenes in Suffolk. Richard Wilson was buried in Mold. It was during the last decade of the 18th century that J M W Turner made an oil painting of Castell Dolbadarn and in the 19th century a water colour of Llanberis Lake. He toured and painted extensively in Gwynedd at the end of the 18th century. He was influenced to some extent by the work of Wilson.

THE BALA LAKE AND THE FAIRBOURNE AND BARMOUTH RAILWAYS

The Bala Lake Railway runs from Llanuwchllyn along the shores of Llyn Tegid to Bala. The first train on the restored line ran in 1972 with diesel locos while steam engines were brought in after 1975. An attraction for tourists and enthusiasts it is longer than the Fairbourne and Barmouth which was originally a horse tramway in the 1880's. This 2 mile (3.2km) line from Fairbourne to Penrhyn Point, the embarkation point for ferries across the Mawddach Estuary to Barmouth was a venture to develop Fairbourne as a seaside resort.

ABERDYFI

The road as well as the railway goes to Machynlleth from Aberdyfi, once a busy port like Abermaw, now a quiet resort. It has the advantage of an extensive sandy beach, pleasant inland walks and facilities for fishing, boating and sailing. Great Britain's first *Outward Bound* school was opened at Aberdyfi in 1944. It can claim a significant place in the history of Wales because, in 1216 Llywelyn ap Iorwerth called a meeting of all the Welsh princes at Aberdyfi. They all pledged their allegiance to him and acknowledged him as their leader and gave him the title, Llywelyn the Great.

CENTRE FOR ALTERNATIVE TECHNOLOGY

In a totally different way from Portmeirion the Alternative Technology Centre shares the theme of care for resources. To have two nuclear power stations would qualify the area as 'advanced' but the most forward-looking project, the major pointer to the new millennium, is this most extensive display of alternative technology in Europe. Open every day, visitors can see displays of organic food-growing, bees, solar power devices, windmills and energy-saving ideas and techniques. One needs a few hours to appreciate the work of the centre off the main A487 road 3 miles (4.8km) north of Machynlleth. It is included in the Cambrian Coast Railway brochure.

Today only Pwllheli and Machynlleth stations are staffed. Normally six sprinter trains leave Pwllheli daily and six arrive; supplying a connection with Machynlleth and from there to Aberystwyth or Birmingham. The company is called Central Trains Ltd, National Express holding the franchise.

THE WELSH HIGHLAND RAILWAY

Designed specifically as a tourist attraction a narrow gauge railway was built from Dinas near Llanwnda along a scenic route through Waunfawr and Betws Garmon reaching Rhyd Ddu in 1881. In 1923 it was extended through Beddgelert to Porthmadog. When the name of Rhyd-ddu station was changed to Snowdon Station to attract more passengers in 1894 it galvanized the people of Llanberis into action. Market forces were at work. Assheton Smith, squire of the mansion, the Faenol, near Y Felinheli, was the important landowner in the Llanberis area. Over many years there were attempts to secure his co-operation to build a railway up Snowdon as a tourist attraction but all to no avail. But in 1894 he gave in. In contrast, as early as 1801, Lord Penrhyn had foreseen the potential of the tourist trade by building the Royal Hotel in Capel Curig. For many years this has been developed into the outdoor pursuits centre Plas y Brenin. Even earlier, possibly, the shrewd landlord of the Goat in **Beddgelert** (Gelert's Grave) had adapted the international folk tale, the great story about Gelert, King Llywelyn's dog which his master had killed in error. Llywelyn had left his faithful friend in a room to guard his baby in a cradle and on his return, finding the cradle overturned and blood on the floor, he impetuously killed Gelert. Within a few minutes he heard a cry from under the cradle and saw a dead wolf in the corner. Prichard the landlord went to the extent of erecting a gravestone to mark the spot where the dog had been buried. It is in a delightful place along a level path within walking distance of the village. It has been recorded that a hillock nearby was known as 'Bryn y Bedd' and suggested that the original Celert was a man of royal lineage.

The life of the Welsh Highland Railway came to an end in 1937, as it seemed for ever, but there has recently been a public enquiry into a project to open the line through Rhyd Ddu to Beddgelert and Porthmadog once more. The Welsh Highland Light Railway 1964 Ltd has been running a train during the summer months for about a mile in Porthmadog and they have interesting exhibits at the Centre. In 1997 a short railway, using the old Caernarfon Afonwen route was opened between Caernarfon and Dinas by a subsidiary of the Ffestiniog Railway Company which is also responsible for the new venture. An indication of the energy and perseverance of the enthusiasts is the fact that locomotives and rails have been brought from South Africa.

THE SNOWDON MOUNTAIN RAILWAY

To return to Llanberis, in 1894, a company was formed to build a railway from the village to the summit of Snowdon, The Snowdon Tramroad and Hotels Co Ltd. The Snowdon Mountain Railway is one of the wonders of Wales and is unique in the British Isles being the only public rack and pinion railway and the highest piece of track measuring 3,493ft (1,064m). The track, nearly 5 miles (8km) long, was laid down in the amazing time of seventy two days. Soon after setting out, and passing the tumbling waterfall of Ceunant Mawr passengers can see the village of Llanberis and Lake Padarn below, and begin to feel the thrill of heights. After Halfway station it becomes really exciting; on the left the challenging ragged edge of Crib Goch above and deep down below, the narrowing Pass of Llanberis; on the right, where the Llanberis path goes under the railway at Clogwyn station, the steep, threatening Clogwyn Du'r Arddu and Llyn Du'r Arddu. The summit is soon within reach; from the top it is a great experience to see mountains, slopes and lakes in all directions, and on a clear day not only distant parts of North Wales but also the Irish Sea, the hills of Wicklow and those of Cumbria and the Isle of Man.

Most passenger trains comprise a locomotive and one coach with a capacity of fifty nine passengers. The loco runs chimney (or bonnet) first up the mountain pushing the coach in front. The coach is not coupled to the locomotive. There are now nine locomotives on the line, five steam and four diesels. Four of the steam locomotives were built in 1895-96 and one in 1922-23. The first two diesels arrived at Llanberis in 1986 followed by two more in 1991 and 1992. A 3-coach diesel-electric railcar set was acquired in 1995.

The line is single track with passing places at Hebron, Halfway and Clogwyn. Laid to a gauge of 800mm or 2ft 7.5ins, it is fitted throughout with a double bladed rack to the design patented by Doctor Abt in 1882. With the exceptions of the tracks in the engine shed and the sidings at Llanberis, there is not one inch of level track on the railway. The average gradient is 1:7.8 and the steepest is 1:5.5. For such steep gradients the rack and pinion principle is used. A cogged wheel on the locomotive engages the indented bar on the track. Coming down it serves as a controlling brake and the system is very safe.

The trains cover the journey from Llanberis to Summit Station in approximately one hour. Each train waits empty at the summit for half an hour before leaving again for the descent to Llanberis. The downhill journey also lasts one hour making a total of two and a half hours for the round trip.

A daily service is operated (weather permitting) throughout the season with departures half hourly during the day subject to there being sufficient passengers. Excursions by coach from Llandudno, Rhyl, Prestatyn and Pwllheli to Llanberis (including the ascent of Snowdon on the railway) operate throughout most of the season which is from 15 March to 1 November inclusive. On fine days, especially in July, August and September, almost all trains are filled to capacity and intending passengers are advised to arrive as early as possible in the day. The telephone number is 01286-870223.

Y Grib Goch

Gwynedd County Council

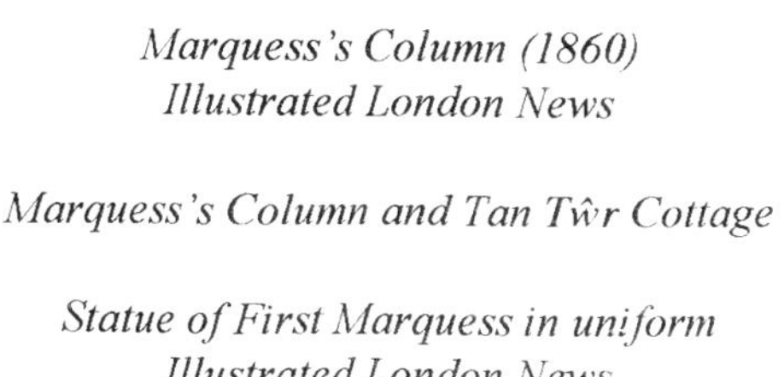

Marquess's Column (1860)
Illustrated London News

Marquess's Column and Tan Tŵr Cottage

Statue of First Marquess in uniform
Illustrated London News

LLANFAIR PWLLGWYNGYLL

THE MARQUESS OF ANGLESEY'S COLUMN

The column, on a hill, on the Menai Bridge side of the village, was built to commemorate Henry William Paget of Plas Newydd, the commander of the Allied Cavalry and second in command to Wellington at the battle of Waterloo 18 June 1815. In that battle near the village of Mont St Jean in Belgium and a little to the South of Waterloo, Napoleon was finally defeated.

Paget lost his leg in the battle. This is how the present Marquess wrote about the incident: 'His right leg was smashed by a cannon ball as he was riding off the field with the Duke at the end of the day. Looking down at his shattered limb he exclaimed, By God, sir, I've lost my leg". To which the Duke, momentarily taking his telescope from his eye, replied, "By God, sir, so you have!" at once resuming his scrutiny of the retreating French'. The number of men killed or wounded on the battlefield was 45,000.

THE FIRST MARQUESS OF ANGLESEY

Paget was honoured for his prominent part in the battle by being made Marquess of Anglesey, the first to bear the title. The old soldier, turned politician, survived for nearly forty years with one foot, literally, in the grave. He died in 1854 aged eighty six.

The total height of the column, erected in 1816, is 112ft (34m). The column and the base are 100ft (30.5m) high and the statue is 12ft (3.4m). The grey marble stones were brought from Moelfre near Benllech by sea to Pwllfanog, the little port half a mile (0.6km) from the village. The architect was Thomas Harrison of Chester and the work was completed in 1817.

THE STATUE

Five years after the death of the first Marquess it was felt that he should be further commemorated. Through the efforts of his son, Admiral Clarence Paget and friends, a statue of the soldier, in his uniform as Colonel of the Seventh Hussars was made. The work in bronze was executed at the studio of the sculptor Mathew Noble in London, probably by a Welshman, Joseph Edwards of Merthyr Tydfil in Glamorgan.

The statue, weighing between two and three tons, was erected on 24 November 1860, according to the plans of a local man Mr Haslam who lived in the small mansion Carreg Brân nearby. The wagon to transport the statue from the station to the site was made locally in the workshop of the carpenter Robert Jones at Bryn Salem.

It is possible to climb to the top of the column up the spiral staircase with 115 steps, tickets being available at **Tŷ Tŵr** at its foot. There is a car park below the rocks on which the column stands, a suitable place for a picnic. It is very convenient to walk from the car park to see the tollhouse, showing the old toll charges, adjacent to the present home of the Women's Institute. The original WI summer house at the private house, Graig, is a few yards up the road. These points of interest are about 200yds (183m) from the Tourist Information Office at the village centre.

THE NELSON MONUMENT

On the foreshore, about 100yds (91m) from St Mary's churchyard, which extends to within a few metres of the high tide level, stands the statue of Lord Nelson often surrounded by water. Near the church, past the country hotel Carreg Brân, there is a car park. This is a convenient place to take a close look at the railway bridge and there is a path down to the water's edge.

Lord Clarence Paget (1811-1895), the son of the first Marquess, was an Admiral who had been in charge of the Mediterranean fleet and was Navy Secretary (1859-1866). In 1853 he was the owner of the mansion, Plas Llanfair. Until 1995 the home of the boys' training school, the TS Indefatigable was there. The land goes down to the Menai Straits. It is now a military training establishment taking advantage of the sea and the rough terrain in the mountains not far away. Lord Clarence was interested in painting and art and he himself, with the help of a local workman, John Jones, made the statue of Nelson in reinforced concrete. His father, the army man, had been nobly honoured. He probably felt that the Navy also needed a tribute.

PLAS NEWYDD (NEW MANSION) NATIONAL TRUST PROPERTY

Plas Newydd (telephone: 01248 714795) is about 1 mile (1.6 km) SW of Llanfair on the A4080 Newborough road. The original house whose name was Llwyn y Moel and the estate belonged to Morfudd, the daughter of Goronwy ap Tudur of Penmynydd whose uncle was the great grandfather of Henry VII or Henry Tudor. Lord Uxbridge, who died in 1812, had made great alterations to the house and had engaged Humphrey Repton to produce one of his famous Red Books for the layout of the park and gardens in 1799. It was after his death that the estate was inherited by Henry William Paget, the first Marquess of Anglesey.

In 1976, the seventh Marquess, Henry, gave the house with its principal contents and 169 acres of garden, park and woodland to the National Trust.

The fourth Marquess (1880-1898), who was a keen cricketer made a first class cricket ground in the park. He was followed by the eccentric fifth Marquess who converted the chapel into a theatre. It was called The Gaiety Theatre and Plas Newydd was known as Anglesey Castle. He used to arrange ambitious productions involving actors and actresses from London with the Marquess himself often taking the leading roles. He spent enormous sums of money on clothes and jewellery and became bankrupt in 1904.

Inside the house the most attractive feature is the very large mural painting by Rex Whistler, while possibly the most interesting object is an articulated artificial limb designed by James Potts of Northumberland for the first Marquess and which was the prototype for others and became known as 'the Anglesey leg'.

There are two remarkable megaliths in the park, the Plas Newydd cromlech or dolmen and Bryn yr Hen Bobl. In the first the huge stones of the New Stone Age tomb are exposed and Bryn yr Hen Bobl (The Mound of the Ancient People) is a covered tomb or chambered cairn which was partially excavated in 1929. Amongst the numerous finds were stone axes from Graig Lwyd, Penmaen-mawr, a honestone, a 14 inch (35.5cm) long block of local grit, that had been used for polishing axes, and charcoal, mainly from hazel.

The present Marquess and the Marchioness still live in a part of Plas Newydd. Lord Anglesey, as well as being the author of authoritative books on military history, has successfully introduced television programmes. Lady Anglesey, the daughter of the English prose writer, Charles Morgan and Hilda Vaughan the novelist from Builth Wells has been Chairperson of the National Federation of Women's Institutes and of the Welsh Arts Council. She is currently a trustee of The Pilgrim Trust, endowed by Mr Harkness an American philanthropist in 1930, and Vice President of the City and Guilds examination awarding body.

THE TAILOR AND THE FUTURE QUEEN

The best true story from Llanfair Pwllgwyngyll concerns a Wesleyan who was a lay preacher and a tailor by trade. His name was John Jones.

In 1832 Princess Victoria aged thirteen and her mother were staying at Plas Newydd. On a Saturday she had a slight accident to her riding habit and a message was sent to seek the assistance of a local tailor. He understood that he was to ask for the Lord Chamberlain of the Household but finding no-one to answer to the title he returned home. On Sunday morning a messenger came once more asking him to

The Old Church Llanfair Pwllgwyngyll before 1850

St Mary's Church today *Photo Mrs Gwenda Williams*

Llandysilio (Church Island) Porthaethwy

come at once but he excused himself explaining that he was just about to go to chapel. Yet another messenger came at mid-day but he had to apologize once more as he was setting out to preach in Red Wharf Bay.

On Monday morning a messenger came again. John Jones was summoned to the presence of the house steward who was very angry. 'Why did you not come yesterday?' He was very dismissive of the lay preacher's reasons. 'Chapel indeed, and preaching! Didn't you know that there was a small job to be done for Her Royal Highness Princess Victoria?' 'I never work on a Sunday, sir'. 'What', said the steward, 'You refused to do a little job for the future Queen of Britain?' 'Well', said Jones, 'Although I am a mere tailor here in Llanfair I expect to be a king in the next world and it would be better for me to lose the respect of the princes of this world rather than forfeit my crown in the next'. This floored the steward. The garment was produced and the repair job done. When it was finished he was told that the Duchess and the Princess were very pleased with his work and his behaviour and if ever he desired a favour at their hands they would be pleased to help him.

ST MARY'S CHURCH LLANFAIR PWLLGWYNGYLL

The present church was built in 1851-52 in the neo-Gothic style fashionable at the time, an attempt to revive architectural features found in 13th century churches. The distinguishing characteristics are the tall spire with the high-pitched roof to match, the buttresses, the tracery on the windows and the pointed arch.

THE OLD CHURCH

The new and larger church was built on the site of an older one. In the journal, *Archaeologia Cambrensis* for 1847 there is a description of the old church, 'the only medieval building in the parish'. 'The building has a circular apse at the eastern end; and hence it may be inferred that the chancel, at least, is a portion of the original building erected before the Anglo-Norman Conquest of the country'.

It is claimed that this apse or semi-circular gable end is unique in Anglesey and in the same journal for 1930 it is said that there was no other example in Caernarfonshire either. It is referred to as 'this foreign Italian plan'.

The earliest known reference to Pwllgwyngyll is in an ecclesiastical document *The Valuation of Norwich* 1254 indicating that a church existed in Llanfair at that time. It is reasonable to assume that it dates from an earlier period and there is archaeological evidence to support that possibility. A case can be made that it dates from the 6th or 7th century, thereby providing a reason why it was remote from whatever settlement there existed at the time. Many churches in Wales were founded by missionary Celtic monks, often referred to as saints, after about 500

AD. Notable examples in Anglesey are Penmon, Caergybi (Holyhead) and Llangwyfan near Aberffraw. E G Bowen in *The Settlement of the Celtic Saints in Wales* has shown that these early Christians preferred isolated places. Their emphasis was on prayer and an ascetic way of life rather than on preaching. It is probable that the monk, on his own or perhaps with two or three others, conducted services in the very tiny church. He was a holy man of noble birth able to influence the chieftain and his family. It is not known how the Christian faith spread amongst the British Celts who had been used to worship their pagan gods and probably persisted in their traditional beliefs. But the sacraments of baptism and holy communion, the burial services and the teaching and example of the saints were a powerful influence on their lives. Over the centuries, the beliefs of the old Celtic religion had rooted firmly and its priests, the druids, were men of great influence but nevertheless the Celtic saints succeeded in winning over the Brythons to Christianity.

LLANDYSILIO
THE ISLAND CHURCH AT PORTHAETHWY (MENAI BRIDGE)

The plain stone building, dating from the 15th century, is situated on a small island on the Llanfair side of the Menai Suspension Bridge. It stands on the site where the Celtic saint Tysilio from Powys established a church at the beginning of the 7th century, probably a very small and simple construction. Until 1926 the church was under the charge of the Rector of Llanfair Pwllgwyngyll, so there is some basis in fact for the Llandysilio in the long name.

It is a pleasant walk through the Coed Cyrnol woods, from the car park opposite the Police Station in Menai Bridge, to the shore. There is a convenient road to the church which is quite near and then to the delightful promenade built by Belgian refugees during the first World War leading under the Suspension Bridge. It is really interesting to see the strong tide running over and past the rocks. There are ideal places to rest near the pier and the bowling green with a number of hotels, restaurants and cafes nearby.

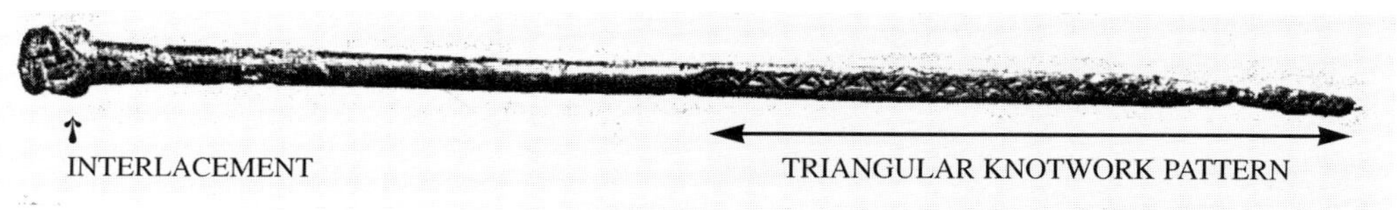

Bronze pin from Llanfair Churchyard

Religious Service - hymn sandwich.

LLANFAIR PWLLGWYNGYLL - THE NAME

The name of the village is the same as that of the parish church. Llanfair means the church of St Mary, one of many bearing the same name from the Middle Ages. The oldest churches were named after the Celtic saints or their patrons who founded them such as St David, St Seiriol and St Tysilio. Later it became customary to adopt the names of saints of the Roman Catholic church so that during the 10th and 11th centuries many were dedicated to St Michael while by the 12th the veneration of Mary became popular.

LLAN

There are two words for 'church' in Welsh, 'eglwys' from the Latin 'ecclesia' and 'llan' which occurs in so many place-names. The original meaning of 'llan' was 'an enclosure'. It occurs in the following compound words; coedlan (copse), ydlan (rickyard), gwinllan (vineyard) and corlan (fold), all enclosures for growing produce, storage or control. In this context it meant the plot of land for Christian burial near the monk's humble dwelling or cell by a well together with his vegetable and fruit garden. Eventually a church would be built and over the years the word 'llan' became synonymous with 'church'.

PWLLGWYNGYLL - THE POOL OF THE WHITE HAZELS

In 1254 in the ecclesiastical document *The Valuation of Norwich* there is a reference to 'piwllgunyl' and in 1333 in *The Record of Caernarfon* a more correct spelling 'Pwllgwigill'.

In *Rhaniadau'r Oesoedd Canol* (The Land Divisions of the Middle Ages) in *Atlas Môn* edited by Melville Richards we can see the boundaries of Llanfair Pwllgwyngyll which correspond quite closely to those of the present parish. Within this area of land are shown two divisions called 'tref' viz. Pwllgwyngyll and Treforion. The word 'tref' here stands for a piece of land with some dwellings; there were two types, land with a small number of farmhouses belonging to free men and the village, consisting of the rude dwellings of the bondmen including arable land on which they laboured. It is thought that the second part of 'Treforion' is the name of one 'Morion' or 'Borion' a free man whose family land was situated somewhere near Tŷ Mawr or Hen Dŷ between Llanfair and Porthaethwy. The history books claim that there were prehistoric terraces in that land sloping towards the Menai Straits. Part of the significance of that is that it is reasonable to assume that it was cultivated for growing grain during the Middle Ages, many centuries later.

The medieval hamlet of Pwllgwyngyll seems to have been near where the old or upper village is today. That suggests that there had been a settlement in that position from the Middle Ages within reach of the arable land of the landowner, probably the Bishop of Bangor and in former times close to Craig y Dinas, the ancient fortified position of a tribe. However it must be borne in mind that the oldest surviving buildings are less than two hundred years old and that the primitive dwellings would have been built of perishable materials, timber, reeds or straw and turf which have long disappeared. The serfs or peasants were responsible also for keeping in good repair the weir Ynys Gorad Goch used for catching fish.

GWYNGYLL - WHITE HAZELS

Usually it is necessary to distinguish a plant by its colour when there is a variety having a different colour e.g. in Welsh 'wermod lwyd', wormwood (grey) and 'wermod wen', feverfew (white wormwood); hawthorn and black thorn. It could be surmised that the same phenomenon is responsible for the term 'white hazel' as there is another variety with red leaves grown as an ornamental shrub. The Latin name for the white hazel is Corylus Avellana, the second part being derived from a place-name in Campania in Italy noted for growing nuts and fruit. The name of the red variety is Corylus Maxima var. Atro purpurea. But it was not until 1759 that this was brought to Britain although the Welsh word 'gwyngyll' existed centuries earlier.

In *Geiriadur Prifysgol Cymru* (University of Wales Dictionary of the Welsh Language) the equivalent English form 'white hazel' is given with the explanation, 'a type of hazel whose pliable shoots are used for making sticks, fishing rods, hoops etc'. The word occurs in a love poem from the 15th century:

> Ar ael mainc hir wiail Mai
> Cuddygl **gwyngyll** a'm cuddiai.

(On the edge of a bench (where I sat) the long branches of the month of May formed a cubicle of white hazels to hide me).

Earlier in the Welsh Laws there is a reference to 'a deuddeg o **wyngyll** a gywerthai â phymtheg ceiniog' (and twelve white hazels are valued at fifteen pence). These were probably straight rods, green for hurdle-making or dried as measuring rods or spears.

In *Y Brython* 1861 in a note about the parish of Beddgelert there is a reference to 'ogof llanciau Eryri' (the cave of the lads of Snowdonia). There was a tradition in the district claiming that Arthur's knights were sleeping in the cave awaiting the return of their leader to regain the crown of Britain, 'because the old true saying is that it will be the young men of Snowdonia and their white hazels who shall win it'. This clearly refers to spears.

If the 'white' in 'gwyngyll' specifically refers to the colour, white, a linguistic explanation is possible. The Brythonic language which developed into Welsh was very similar to the Celtic of Gaul. In southern Europe the red variety of hazel was indigenous so it was necessary to call the other one white to distinguish between them. The name could have come with the language of the invaders, later developing into Welsh. The corresponding Old Irish name is *findchuill, find* meaning 'white'.

But in Welsh 'gwyn' in a metaphoric sense was used for 'beautiful, lovely, holy and blessed'. The last two adjectives have a Christian connotation so it is conceivable that 'sacred, secret' would apply equally well in connection with the former Celtic religion. Our ancestors' belief in the virtue of the hazel is relevant and interesting as we shall see.

In *The Celtic Tree Oracle* by Liz and Colin Murray it is claimed that the hazel was associated with contemplation and the power to solve disputes. The tree and the nuts are represented by the colour brown.

In the Irish primitive alphabet 'ogham', consisting of notches carved on wood or stone, the marks corresponded to Latin letters and to features in nature. An ogham mark stood for 'c' and the hazel (collen).

In folklore there are references to the virtues of the hazel and it is probable that the magician's magic wand would be a hazel stick in its natural state or decorated in some way.

ATTEMPTS TO EXPLAIN THE NAME LLANFAIR PWLLGWYNGYLL

The explanation so far accepted is the interesting one proposed by Sir John Morris-Jones. First of all, it is useful to take a quick look at the earliest history of Anglesey. As in other parts of Europe the first trees in our country were birch and Scots pine (c. 10,000 - 8,000 BC). By about 7,000 - 6,000 BC the hazel had established itself and then oak, alder and ash. The natural home of the Old Stone Age people was the forest which covered most of the land. At that time, until around 6,000 BC Anglesey was attached to the mainland, Ireland to Britain and Britain in its turn to Europe.

A WHIRLPOOL IN THE MENAI

A fascinating insight into the nature of the landscape is given in a story related by Sir John Morris-Jones in 1926. He could recall, forty years earlier, when men were draining the marshland between Llanfair station and Aber Braint, that about a foot or eighteen inches (30-46cms) down through the clay they came upon a layer of about four to six inches thick (10-15cms) of hazel nuts in a sort of soft clay. He came to the conclusion that the whole district was at one time covered with hazel trees and that there were so many of them as to ascribe to the whole area this particular feature. And when it became necessary to name the whirlpool in the Menai, this dominant feature presented itself giving Pwllgwyngyll.

This hypothesis is supported by the name of another whirlpool in the Menai, Pwll Ceris, near the Suspension Bridge, otherwise known as the Swellies, notorious as a danger to shipping. It was here that the famous old sailing ship HMS *Conway* was driven on to the rocks, the Swelly Rock and the Platters, in 1953. And Pwll Ceris is not the only one in the vicinity. The name of the little harbour near Llanfair is Pwllfanog but that is not its correct name. In 1536-1539 (John Leland, *Collecteana*) the name is 'Aberpwllfanogl' and in 1710 Henry Rowlands (1655-1723), who was not a reliable etymologist, gave 'Aber y pwll y ffanoge'. Aber means 'estuary'.

Dr Cecil Jones of the University of Wales, Bangor and others have conducted under-water research near Pwllfanog. Having confirmed that there was a dock on the Anglesey side from at least 1500 AD he is convinced that there was another one on the opposite side. The evidence consists of old anchors and wrecks. The sea bed, on the Arfon side, some distance from the shore drops sharply. According to E Greenly, the authority on the geology of Anglesey, after the Ice Age there was a waterfall from one of the mountain rivers at this spot. Today there is a deep hole, well known to fishermen, about 100ft (30.4m) deep. It is conceivable that this is Pwllfanog although there is a pool at the mouth of the River Braint.

In passing it is as well to note that the incoming tides from the Penmon and Caernarfon ends of the Straits do not meet near the two bridges but near Gallows Point, Beaumaris.

There is evidence therefore supporting the theory that 'Pwllgwyngyll' refers to a whirlpool near the Llanfair (Britannia) Bridge. But after all it is conjecture. Incidentally the discovery of the layer of nuts was made near Llyn y Felin (the mill pool) which used to be near where the station is now. However the records show this as 'llyn' (lake) not 'pwll' (pool), and there used to be a smallholding nearby called Glan Llyn.

A POOL BY THE CHURCH

It is necessary to consider another possibility. 'Pwll' is commonly used as the English 'pool' for standing water on land. It is not unexpected that by the old rectory, near St Mary's church, there is a well by the side of the road. On the other side of the wall there is a wet patch where there used to be a duckpond being fed by the well and also by a little stream from another direction. These remain despite the building of a railway embankment within yards. There was a spring in Pant Lodge field and a stream that ran under Carreg Brân. The stream reappears in the churchyard. Perhaps the pool of which all that remained was the duckpond, had been a significant feature.

The well by the church has been called 'Ffynnon Sadwrn' and 'Ffynnon Ddu' (black). Until the early part of the 20th century old residents believed that there was some medicinal value in its water.

The two names are interesting. There is no mention of a Celtic saint connected with Llanfair church but it is quite possible that Sadwrn, the founder of Llansadwrn, a neighbouring church, established it. It was common practice for a number of wells to be dedicated to one saint or benefactor. There are many St David's in Pembroke and there are three for St Seiriol, at Penmon, Llaniestyn and one of the Clorach wells in the parish of Llandyfrydog opposite St Cybi's well. There is a tradition that St Seiriol would walk, starting in the morning, from Penmon towards the centre of Anglesey, with the sun to his back while St Cybi would come to meet him from Holyhead facing the sun. So they were called Seiriol Wyn (white) and Cybi Felyn (tanned). This raises the possibility that Cybi was really a foreigner of dark skin. It is said that, initially, the lower stone walls near the well in Penmon, were part of Seiriol's tiny church in the 6th century. That would make it the oldest remaining Christian building in Wales. This story about Seiriol and Cybi meeting at the well of Clorach is well known but there is also a tradition that another monk, Eilian, used to meet them having walked from the promontory at Point Lynas or **Llaneilian**. As one would expect there is a well associated with the name of Eilian about half a mile from the church, the most interesting in Anglesey. Most of the present building is from the 12th century including the distinctive tower. The interesting features inside are the rood screen, the very small Eilian's chapel and Eilian's oak chest for pilgrims' offerings. It has been suggested that Lynas, in Welsh 'Leinws', is derived from *Eilianus.*

To build a church near a well made sense because water was needed for drinking and baptizing. If Sadwrn consecrated the well in Llanfair and that it was his name that was originally associated with the church, it would be quite feasible to suppose that his name was replaced by that of Mary during the Middle Ages as happened in many instances under the influence of the Roman Catholic Church. The gravestone of Sadwrn, now inside Llansadwrn church, is dated c. 500 AD.

But what about 'Ffynnon Ddu', the black well? Could 'black' be a pejorative adjective used by the Christians to describe the well that had previously been sacred under the old Celtic religion? Some wells are called 'Ffynnon y Wrach' (the witch's well), 'gwrach' referring to the pagan priestesses of the Celts. Francis

Jones in *The Holy Wells of Wales* mentions 'Ffynnon Chwerthin' (Laughing Well) in Llanberis where the bog shakes causing bubbles and says that this was attributed to 'the old black boys, the servants of the witches'. If these were the beliefs of the pagans, to the Christian leaders they were the dark superstitions of the devil and it took centuries for the country people to forget them.

A HOLY PLACE?

Why was Llanfair church built at this spot near the Menai? Was it considered sacred? In folklore there are stories about goblins obstructing the building of churches in inappropriate places by demolishing the masons' work during the night implying that they were regarded as sacred. Bearing in mind that the Celts had their own gods and religious rites under the influence of the druids one can imagine that there was considerable resistance to the Christian monks. Perhaps there is an echo of the conflict in the account in *The Life of St David* of the opposition to St David by the Irish king Boia and significantly there is a well and hazel nuts in that story as well.

Francis Jones in *The Holy Wells of Wales* wrote, 'It has been noted that the church decreed that pagan sites were to be converted to Christian solemnities and this the missionaries did by rededicating the well, the megalith and the tree and by erecting churches or chapels near them'. Rather than destroying venerated places and antagonizing people they adopted them and Christianized them.

If there were hazel trees growing near a pool in the vicinity of the church that would constitute a powerful combination of features held sacred in the Celtic religion. Could that, after all, be the 'Pwllgwyngyll'? The mystery remains.

SACRED WATER - MAGIC HAZELS

We have now touched upon an interesting aspect of the history of the Celts. The subject has been studied by well-known scholars such as Norah Chadwick, Frances Lynch and others and in this specific field by Anne Ross. In *Pagan Celtic Britain* she discusses sacred places at length. There are three sources of information on which her studies are based; the work of Roman writers, archaeology and the ancient tales in the mythical literature of Ireland and Wales.

The Celts regarded pools, lakes and wells as entrances to the other world and it was a custom among them to place valuable equipment and treasures into the water as a votive offering to the gods. That is considered to account for the important discovery of bronze and iron objects at Llyn Cerrig Bach near Valley, Anglesey during the 1939-45 war. It has been suggested that they were deposited there after the Romans invaded Anglesey in 60 AD and that they remained in good condition as they were embedded in the peat. Wells and deep pits were similarly venerated. Anne Ross gives an account of an interesting shaft at Ashill, Norfolk. It is a hole 40ft (12m) deep, 3.5ft (1m) square. In the first 19ft (5.8m) there were pieces of pottery, painted wall plaster, bones, part of a wooden bucket, a basket, an iron knife and so on. Lower down the contents changed. Dr Ross wrote 'They now consisted of fairly perfect urns placed in layers and embedded in leaves of hazel and hazel nut'.

She points out how special the hazel was in old Irish literature, not only in the respect for the tree but in its constant association with sacred wells. By the well of Connla, under the sea, the hazel of wisdom grew and the magical nuts fell into the water. Then the sacred salmon ate them and so partook of their supernatural wisdom. The well is mentioned in *Celtic Heritage* by Alwyn and Brinley Rees: 'This well was the source of inspiration and knowledge. Over it grew nine hazels of wisdom "out of which were obtained the feats of the sages" '. The hazel nuts dropped into the well and caused bubbles of mystic inspiration to form on the stream that issued from it. In another tale hazel nuts are used as love charms.

FOLKLORE

In the folklore of different countries the hazel was held in high regard on account of its magical qualities. It was the water diviner's favourite twig and there were more auspicious times to cut one, Good Friday or the midsummer feast of St John, 24 June. This suggests a pre-Christian connection, pre-Celtic in fact, with the Summer Solstice feast 21 June. To witness the remarkable phenomenon of a forked twig bending and vibrating in the hands of the water diviner, and then to discover water at that spot, would confirm people's belief that the person was under the influence of some supernatural power or god.

At the beginning of the 18th century the scholar Edward Lhuyd published a comprehensive survey of the Welsh parishes; unfortunately he did not receive any response at all from the Anglesey clergy. However, under 'Tal y Llyn' Meirionnydd, there is an account of a discovery at Llwyn Dôl Ithel, of a carved wooden coffin with the skeleton of a man and a woman. There were other graves. It was noticed that hazel rods, a yard and half long, with the bark on them had been put by the sides of the coffins.

Old folk customs illustrate the fact that the hazel could bring a blessing and good luck. One custom that was widespread in Europe was to present the bride with the gift of a bag of nuts as the married couple came out of the church. In France hazel nuts were thrown at the bride and groom as they knelt at the altar, an act similar to the throwing of rice and nowadays confetti.

How old were these beliefs then? After excavation at Bryn yr Hen Bobl, (Plas Newydd) during 1929-35, analysis showed that the wood remains were mostly oak but second came hazel and what is more significant, they found the remains of two nuts. At Bryn Celli Ddu also there were plenty of hazel remains. At the bottom of that burial chamber a branch of hazel and a burnt human ear bone were found. And that goes back to 2,500-2,000 BC long before the time of the Celts. The question is, was the site of Llanfair church decided by the existence of a Celtic or, perhaps, a pre-Celtic place of worship near the well?

A POOL IN THE UPPER VILLAGE

There is another possibility. It has been explained that Pwllgwyngyll was a medieval township which was an area of land together with the clustered houses of the peasants. If this was the site of the present upper village, it could also be the location of the pool of the white hazels. There is a field called Cae Gorswen (white marsh field) and it seems that Gorswen was an alternative name for the upper village. Near Tyddyn Deici there was, until 1925, a marsh and a fairly large pool where children used to skate in winter. It is possible that the white hazels grew by this pool.

These seem feasible alternatives until some documentary or archaeological evidence is found that decides the matter.

A CELTIC CHURCH

Leaving aside the matter of the pool of the white hazels, there is some evidence that the original church was founded during the age of the Celtic saints. As mentioned before there is documentary evidence about the church going back to 1254. In the early years of the 20th century, Mr William Pritchard, Garnedd Wen, Llanfair, discovered a bronze pin in the graveyard. It was found about 9ft (2.7m) down while digging a grave in the lower part of the graveyard. Sir Cyril Fox classified it as an Irish pin of the 10th century. It is reasonable to deduce that it was put there in connection with an early burial. That goes back to c. 900 AD although it does not follow that the grave was as old as the pin. But it is reasonable to assume that the church and burial ground had been in the same place for a few centuries.

THE SEA ROUTES

On an old map there is a name for the shore near Llanfair church, Porth Fair (the port of St Mary). During the Middle Ages and for centuries before and after, indeed up to the 18th century, there were in the country only footpaths and rough lanes impassable in winter because of the mud. How essential, then, would have been the coracle, the boat and the ship. They were used for fishing and for travelling and especially for transporting goods. At Porth Fair a ship could be anchored and boats could be beached conveniently. In the background, apart from the farmers and their produce, would be the carpenter, the shoemaker, the smith and other craftsmen as well as tradespeople buying and selling tools, utensils and so on. That kind of trade by sea had been carried on for centuries.

If we conjecture correctly that there was a Celtic church in Llanfair it is no wonder that it is in an out of the way cove. The missionary monks sought isolated locations near the sea and the three churches, Llandysilio, Llanfair and Llanedwen are similarly situated.

LLANSADWRN - A GRAVESTONE FROM THE 6TH CENTURY

In attempting to explain the place-name Llanfair Pwllgwyngyll it has been suggested that there is a possibility that the original church was founded in the age of the Celtic saints by Sadwrn the founder of Llansadwrn, the neighbouring village. But the study of personal and place names is difficult and dangerous. In view of the large number of saints beginning with Gwyn or Gwen (female); Gwenfaen, Gwynen, Gwenllwyfo (females), Gwyn, Gwynno, Gwynoro, Gwyndaf, Gwyndeyrn, Gwyngeneu, Gwynhoedl, Gwynio, Gwynnin, Gwynlleu, Gwynllyw, Gwynnog, and Gwynws one wonders whether there could have been a Gwyngyll as well.

On the road from Porthaethwy (Menai Bridge) to Pentraeth about 2 miles (3.2km) from Llanfair there is a crossroads, Merddyn Groes, the right turn going to Llansadwrn with the church on the right before reaching the village. Inside the church, on the north wall, there is a notable stone. It is the gravestone of Sadwrn that was outside in the graveyard until the 18th century. The letters of some of the Latin words are missing. It is one of the oldest stones in Wales with an inscription and is unique in Wales in one respect. It is the only stone commemorating the founder of a church that has remained on the site where he originally established a church. Scholars have drawn attention to the language and the style of the letters of the inscription. The language is Latin and the stone has been dated to about 500 AD. Although the Romans had left Britain around 400 AD Latin was widely spoken and used, particularly by the ruling classes alongside Welsh which was in the process of development from Brythonic during the period 450-550 AD. When Christianity arrived through the efforts of monks like Dewi, Latin was the medium of education in the religious establishments such as Llanilltud Fawr and Penmon. There is strong evidence that it was from Gaul or France that the main stream of Christianity flowed into our country. From prehistoric times communication by sea had been predominant and it persisted to this period and later. Between the continent, Brittany, Cornwall, Pembroke, Llŷn, Anglesey, Cumbria, Scotland and Ireland this Western sea route was a vital link for many centuries. The Menai Straits afforded suitable sheltered harbours, one of which was Porth Fair just below the churchyard in Llanfair Pwllgwyngyll. The style of the lettering on the Llansadwrn stone shows the influence of similar craftsmanship in Gaul. In view of the evidence of the Irish pin found in the graveyard and that one name ascribed to the well by the church in Llanfair is Ffynnon Sadwrn it is probable that there was a Celtic church in this place. In the 6th century it would have been a very simple wooden construction by the monk's cell, the sacred burial place, a garden and the well.

It is said that Sadwrn was the brother of St Illtyd and a knight. It seems, therefore, that he was a soldier who had, with his wife, dedicated his life to Christianity. Illtyd was a very learned abbot. His monastery at Llanilltud Fawr in the Vale of Glamorgan was the earliest educational establishment in Britain. The monks who were educated there were able to spread Christianity to distant places.

Off the road from Llansadwrn to Llanddona stands what is arguably the most important house in Anglesey, Hafoty, formerly Hafoty Rhydderch. Built in the 14th century it is of the medieval type. The fireplace from around 1530 has a Tudor arch with an inscription, *SI DEUS NOBISCUM QUIS CONTRA NOS* (If God be for us, who can be against us?).

NAMES

AMERICA

The Penguin Dictionary of Surnames claims that the name America is derived from a Welsh person's name.

John Cabot, the sailor and explorer, originally from Genoa, was encouraged in his voyages by King Henry VII (1457-1509), a Welshman, the grandson of Owain Tudur of the Tudor family from Penmynydd, 2 miles (3.2km) from Llanfair, who married Catherine de Valois the young widow of Henry V.

Cabot who discovered Newfoundland in 1497, was backed by merchants from Bristol, the chief of these being a Welshman who was a collector of customs. His name had been Anglicized to 'Richard Ameryk' but had been 'ap Meryk'. As a surname it became, amongst other versions, Meyrick and it spread to the English border counties. Ap (son of) corresponds to the Irish and Scottish 'mac', while

'Yes we must, indeed, all hang together, or most assuredly we shall all hang separately'.
Benjamin Franklin (1706 - 1790). Remark at the signing of the Declaration of Independence.

'Meurig' is still popular as a Christian name. To honour this man who had helped him, Cabot called the new continent America after him.

WELSH PLACE-NAMES

Old maps and documents supply ample evidence of the difficulty that English officials have had in spelling Welsh words. Although Welsh speakers, even children, have no problem with the spelling or the pronunciation one must sympathize with non-Welsh speakers trying to cope with such names as, Llanfair Mathafarn Eithaf, Llanrhaeadr-ym-Mochnant, Llanfihangel Genau'r-glyn, Llanfihangel Bachellaeth and Llanfair Pwllgwyngyll.

In addition to being long they contain the difficult sounds; 'll, th, ch and r'. There are three 'll's in Llanfair Pwllgwyngyll. To the Welsh ear the above are attractive place-names but are extremely difficult for the English tongue.

During the second half of the 19th century more and more people from England were visiting North Wales attracted by the mountains, the beaches, the scenery and the ease of travelling by ship and train. It was a temptation for English postcard publishers to have some fun at the expense of these Welsh names and for the Welsh to pay back in kind by pillorying the English over their mispronunciations.

THE LONG, LONG NAME

LLANFAIRPWLLGWYNGYLLGOGERYCHWYRNDROBWLL-
LLANDYSILIOGOGOGOCH

It was at this time, around 1870, that the famous long name was strung out by the mischievous tailor from the small town of Porthaethwy (Menai Bridge) 1.5 miles (2.4km) from Llanfair.

Although the long name had caught on early it was dismissed as tomfoolery by the famous Welsh scholar Sir John Morris-Jones (1864-1929). He wrote: 'I heard the late John Williams, cabinet maker of Talybont saying that he well remembered the time the ridiculous monstrosity was composed and that it was some doggerel-writing tailor from Menai Bridge who made it up'.

Partly as a result of this condemnation by a man of such authority, no-one thought more about the author of the world-famous long name. Even though articles were published in magazines and papers and items broadcast on radio and television in different countries, no-one had shown an interest in the author of the long name. That is, until September 1996, when two journalists from the Netherlands, on a visit expressed astonishment that nothing was known about the anonymous tailor. They mentioned that there was a letter in the Tourist Office from a lady claiming to be one of his descendants. This was an interesting piece of information. The lady was Mrs Gwen Harding Roberts of Llandrillo yn Rhos (Rhos-on-Sea). Here is an extract from her letter:

'I remember so well our family speaking of my great-grandfather who "invented" the name. He was Hughes the tailor of Menai Bridge who had a shop (very high class!) in Uxbridge Square next door but one to the Midland Bank, Trinity House. This shop later became a butcher's. The old gentleman made yachting suits for the rich yachting crowd of those days. He was on my nain's (granny's) side of the family'.

Mrs Harding Roberts was quite sure of the surname but not the first name; she thought it could be Robert. Being a humorous character he put together the long name as a family joke in the first place. The connection was corroborated by Mrs Gwyn Taylor of Trearddur who is another great grand-daughter.

Mrs Gwen Harding Roberts's letter was a stroke of good luck. Armed with the important surname, his work - a tailor, and the address - Trinity House it was possible to check in the census returns of 1861, 1871 and 1881.

The record for 1871 read:

Beaumaris Road No 2				
Thomas Hughes	Head Mar.	46	Tailor emp. 1 man	Gwalchmai
Anne Hughes	Wife Mar.	40	Tailor	
Jane Hughes	Daur. Unm.	21	Milliner	
Margaret Anne Hughes	Daur. Unm.	15	Dressmaker	
John Henry Hughes	Son	7	Scholar	
Selina May Hughes	Daur.	3		
John Williams	Nephew	16	App. tailor	Liverpool

Number 2 Beaumaris Road is the same place as Trinity House. So the man behind the long name at last had a name and an identity. By 1881 the family had moved to 5 Packet Road when Thomas Hughes was described as a tailor and draper. Mrs Gwyn Taylor could recall later members of the family living there and that it was the late Dr Fisher's house or next door.

With the help of Mr R R Williams, a leading member of the Gwynedd Family History Society and their valuable record of the memorial inscriptions in the graveyard of Llandysilio, Church Island, the grave of Thomas Hughes's family was found; a flat stone on the right near the path leading to the church door. The

Gravestone of Thomas Hughes   Photo Derec Owen

Mrs Gwen Harding Roberts

Daniel Owen and tailors Mold c. 1880   *Flintshire Archives*

daughter of Thomas Hughes, Mrs Margaret Anne Hughes was Mrs Harding Roberts's grandmother. She and her husband, also Thomas Hughes of Bryn Aethwy are buried in the same graveyard.

The testimony of the gravestone of Thomas Hughes who died in 1890 is that they were Welsh-speaking. The hymn inscribed on the stone 'Rwy'n tynnu tuag ochr y dŵr' is by Thomas Williams, Bethesda'r Fro (Glamorgan) (1761-1844) one of the great hymn writers of the 18th century. In the Calvinistic Methodist Hymn Book of 1913 (No 833) it is printed as one stanza but in the current Presbyterian and Wesleyan book it is printed with the well known, 'Adenydd colomen pe cawn' by the same author. However there is some local evidence that the Hughes family was Congregationalist.

Thomas Hughes died in 1890. There may be, somewhere, a photograph of him on his own or in a group. No such picture has come to light as yet. This is surprising for a prosperous, middle class business family of the Victorian period.

SENSE OR NONSENSE?

Fair play to Thomas Hughes, his verbal fabrication does make sense. Looking down from the Marquess's column one can see the elements of the name quite clearly: Llanfair, St Mary's church; Pwllgwyngyll, the pool of the white hazels (somewhere in Llanfair village or the Straits); gogerychwyrndrobwll, near the turbulent whirlpool, (a reference to the notoriously dangerous water near the Swelly rock). Opposite this spot is the island church of Tysilio. 'Gogo' means 'cave' and it has been suggested that this came from another place-name Llandysiliogogo in Cardiganshire. 'Goch' the final syllable probably refers to the prominent feature Ynys Gorad Goch between the two bridges.

JOKE, DEVILMENT, PUBLICITY?

It is true that the long name has been used for publicity but that was not the original intention. Though it started as a family joke the tailor must have been well aware of the difficulty that the extra two 'ch's, two 'll's and three 'r's would cause for English people. Sir John Morris-Jones's indignation suggests that there was some friendly inter-village rivalry.

WORDS, RIDDLES, RHYMES

When we think of family and social life one hundred years ago and more we can imagine that there would be a great deal of conversation on the hearth and in the workplace. As well as news and stories there would be riddles and conundrums for amusement; the spoken word was very important. An indication is found in,

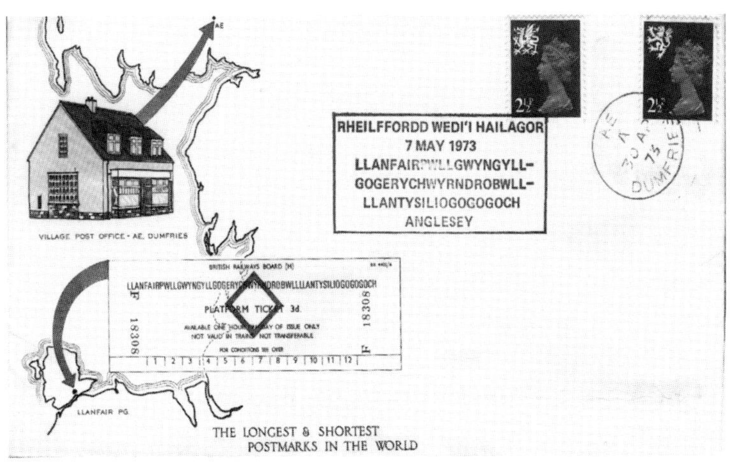

Longest and shortest postmarks *Scotsman Cover Services*

for example, the *Dictionary of Riddles* by Mark Bryant which quotes from another book *Home Amusements* c. 1890, 'A collection of over 400 riddles of various kinds, plus forfeits, parlour games etc'.

Here are some Welsh riddles:

Cist fach yng ngwaelod y nant Agorith un, nis caeith cant.	The small chest's secret who can disclose it? One can open it. A hundred can't close it.
Ateb: cneuen.	***Answer: a nut.***
Beth sy'n mynd ymhell ar ei phen? ***Ateb: hoelen mewn esgid.***	What goes a long way on its head? ***Answer: a nail in a shoe.***
Beth sy'n troi i bob tŷ ar y ffordd i Gaer? ***Ateb: llwybr.***	What turns into every house on the way to Chester? ***Answer: a path.***
An English riddle:	Welsh Proverb:
Y Y U R Y Y U B I C U R Y Y 4 ME	Mud will show However slight, Like a blot on a page If the horse is white.

Whenever people gathered together there would be jokes, tall stories, versifying, and reminiscing. In the Band of Hope and other gatherings centred on the chapels, the children and young people would read aloud, recite and sing and take part in competitions such as reciting tongue twisters, composing oral sentences, the words beginning with the same letter or the letters of a word and reading aloud an unpunctuated passage containing humorous combinations and potential pitfalls. It was against this background that Thomas Hughes, the tailor, composed the long name.

TAILORING AND DRESSMAKING

The life of Thomas Hughes coincided with that of a very well known literary figure, the novelist, Daniel Owen of Mold (1836-1895) who was also a tailor.

This was a time when small towns were very busy places. There were many people engaged in trade and crafts and a great deal of the food, clothes and other necessities were available locally. Old pictures show the streets full of people and horse-drawn vehicles.

During most of the 19th century there was plenty of work for the tailor and dressmaker. It was towards the end of the century that ready-made clothes were becoming widely available. Men of the upper class, and to some extent middle class and even working class on formal occasions, wore three quarter length frock coats and tailcoats as well as shorter jackets called pilot coats or reefers. Top hats and bowlers were fashionable. Long, very full-skirted dresses were the mode for women, from the early crinolines to the popular bustles later. Their dresses and headwear were very elaborate.

LONG NAME - SMALL WORLD

It is estimated that half a million people visit Llanfair Pwllgwyngyll every year. On 30 September 1996 on just one coach calling on the way from Ireland to London there were tourists from Australia, New Zealand, Singapore, British Columbia and the United States of America. Visitors come from different parts of the United Kingdom and Ireland, from the European countries and from the Far East.

The fascination with the long name has been shown in many ways; visitors taking photographs, the production and sending of postcards, much-valued postmarks, requests for pronunciation and attempts to do so, with different degrees of success all over the world, souvenirs and requests for information from many countries.

Ms Irene Dammers Amsterdam

'CONSIDER THE POSTAGE STAMP. ITS USEFULNESS CONSISTS IN THE ABILITY TO STICK TO ONE THING UNTIL IT GETS THERE'. (JOSH BILLINGS) HENRY WHEELER SHAW (1818 - 1885)

Here are some examples of correspondence:

The Public Library
Saskatoon
Saskatchewan
Jan 30 1967

The Worshipful the Mayor

The full name (of the village) was given in the McGraw-Hill International Atlas.

We would very much like to hear about your town as it certainly is unique and our patrons would like to at least have a letter to view from your town.

Of course, our name of Saskatoon is rather unique, being that of a native berry which grows along our river banks. Its origin is Sioux Indian as is our provincial name of Saskatchewan which means 'swift flowing river'. We, of course, would be happy to know the origin of the name of your town.

Yours truly

Wilbur N Lepp
Local History Librarian

This is another example:

Edition du Journal Polonais Lens
NARODOWIEC
Lens
101 rue Emile Zola
March 2nd 1967

The Town Council
Gentlemen

Only now have we heard in France that some frivolous thieves have robbed the town of Lianfairpawligwingigoggeryshwirndrobwillintisilloggogch of the signpost indicating its name. We wish you every success in recovering the property.

Yours faithfully

The Polish daily 'Narodowiec' and its readers (largely miners in France and

Belgium with names as unpronounceable as that of your town).
(This is a reference to one of the occasions when the sign on the railway station had been taken away).

Again:

Amsterdam
The Netherlands

February 1970

Dear sir

Maybe you are surprised to receive a letter from a Dutch girl. But I want to tell you that I have made a remarkable thing, perhaps you will like it. It is an embroidery of the name of your village. I am greatly interested in Wales and I like embroidery and when I found in a little book the longest Welsh place-name, I almost immediately started embroidering it on a strip of sheet. My mother shook her head when I told her this, 'You won't even have finished it when you'll be twenty years old!' and I was seventeen. But when I had finished it I was still seventeen. Now the embroidery hangs over the curtains in my room. I am learning the Welsh language as well as I can; that's not easy but I enjoy it.

My mother has taken some photographs. So you can imagine how my piece of work is.

With kind regards, yours sincerely

Irene Dammers

And this one from Germany:

Werner Dietze
Kreis Geithain
Deutsche Demokratische Republik

To the mayor of the village
Llanfairpwllgwyngyllgogerychwyrndrobwll-llantysiliogogogoch
WALES / Great Britain

Dear Mayor,

I have a very great favour to ask of you! I am a friend of model railways and recently I read in our newspaper or magazine about your village. I could learn that your village has the longest name in the world.

Oh, I was astonished about that long and unpronounceable name. I dare say that you don't take it ill of somebody if he can't pronounce this name. I think this is possible only someone who was born in Wales, isn't it?

Well, Sir, may I say my wish?

I ask you for some pictures from your village especially some with the long name e.g. a photo from your railway station, on which one can see the whole name! Would you do me such a favour? I know that would be a great kindness of you. Already now I thank you very much for your generosity.

Please, be so kind as to send some pictures.

I remain, dear Sir,

Yours very sincerely,
Signed Werner Dietze

PS I enclose two postcards for you from Leipzig the city with the famous fair.

LONGEST PLACE-NAMES

According to the Guinness Book of Records the longest place-name in use is in Southern Hawke's Bay, New Zealand and has eighty five letters: Taumatawhakatangihangakoauauotamateaturipukakapikimaungahoronukupokaiw henuakitanatahu, a hill, the Maori translation meaning: the place where Tamatea, the man with the big knees, who slid, climbed and swallowed mountains, known as landeater, played his flute to his loved one. In England, Saint Mary le More and All Hallows with Saint Leonard and Saint Peter (57 letters, Wallingford, Oxon). In Scotland, Meallan Liath Coire Mhic Dhubhghaill (32 letters, near Aultanrynie, Highland). In the Republic of Ireland, Muckanaghederdauhalia (21 letters near Oughterard, Co Galway), literally meaning the piggery between two briny inlets. The official name for Bangkok, the capital of Thailand, has 175 letters.

With regard to the shortest place-names, there are the villages, AE in Dumfries, Scotland, Ee in Friesland, Y in France, A in Denmark, Norway and Sweden. 'I' is the Gaelic for the island of Iona, off Mull, St Columba's resting place.

ANOTHER CLAIM TO FAME

Thomas Hughes lived from 1826 to 1890. At the same time c.1825-1895, there lived in Porthaethwy another famous character, Y Bardd Cocos (The Cockle Bard). He composed simple verses on a variety of topics stating the obvious and banal. His forte was the end rhyme of which he would include not two but six or seven close together. The one about the stone lions on the Llanfair Bridge is well known and often repeated. It was translated by the Rev T Charles Williams:

Pedwar llew tew	*Four fat lions*
Heb ddim blew	*Without any hair*
Dau'r ochor yma	*Two over this side*
A dau'r ochor drew.	*And two over there.*

He was illiterate but could recite all his verses from memory. Another attempt at translation will illustrate his style:

THE MARQUESS'S STATUE

Marquess of Anglesey,
Lord of the land,
With his sword in his hand;
He can't change hands - that's plain
In the driving rain.

Unorthodox in his ways, outlandish in his appearance and without pattern or parallel in his compositions, the poor fellow was subjected to ridicule by the self-important poets of the eisteddfodau but while most of their 'poetry' has long been forgotten the verses of Bardd Cocos are still well known and continue to entertain. Referring again to the Sphinx-like statues on the Llanfair Bridge he said:

Four lions vain
And full of disdain

Someone asked: 'Why do you call them vain?'

'Oh, they won't turn their heads
Even to look at the train'.

He got the name 'cocos' from one of his occupations which was gathering cockles on Traeth Lafan and selling them. For his work he had a donkey and cart and at

John Evans y Bardd Cocos
(The Cockle Bard)

Mr Medwyn Williams, winner of Gold Medals for vegetable displays, three times in succession at Chelsea, 1996, 1997, 1998, Hampton Court 1996 and Cincinnati, Ohio. At the Chelsea Flower Show 1996 HM The Queen was impressed and shared a joke with Medwyn when he said 'I've got to live there to grow leeks this long'.

A long name postcard

one time he had to get a new cart. 'Surely, 'he said 'I can make a wooden cart if they succeeded in building the Menai Bridge at the first go. He was able to make a rough box but he had to search around Bangor for an axle and wheels. Eventually he was successful but one wheel was bigger than the other. On the road, a passer-by asked him whether it wasn't very awkward driving with different sized wheels. 'It does tend to pull to the side' he said 'but I can always change the wheels'. 'But you'll be pulled to the other side then'. 'Oh no, I have a stronger rein on that side'.

THE WOMEN'S INSTITUTE

Unfortunately the name *The Women's Institute* has acquired the image of a sedate, middle class society for the middle aged and elderly. It is therefore high time to remind ourselves of the origins of the movement which gives a totally different picture.

It was at Stoney Creek near Hamilton on Lake Ontario, Canada, in 1897 that the first branch of the Women's Institute was formed, but the roots were in the soil of Ireland and in the field of agriculture. The middle and second half of the 19th century was a very hard period for rural areas in many countries. Because of the potato famine (1847-8) and its consequences Ireland suffered more than any other country. Seeing the extreme poverty and starvation among farmers, smallholders and peasants, Sir Horace Plunkett thought of a possible remedy, a co-operative movement. The basis of his policy was better farming, better business, a better livelihood. He saw that the farmers themselves had to secure improvements by standing together rather than being at the mercy of landlords and profiteering dealers.

The idea caught on in North America and some countries in Europe while the women's movement in Canada was the child of the Agricultural Society. The pioneers were women facing an extremely hard life and extreme difficulties of travelling. In the words of the old comic song they were 'mighty tough'. In Europe one country that earnestly set about the task of establishing branches was Belgium.

On 20 October 1911 the Irishman Sir Horace Plunkett came to Bangor to address the first meeting of the North Wales branch of the Agricultural Organization Society, the first public meeting to be held in the new building, the Prichard-Jones Hall. The University College of North Wales, Bangor was the first in the United Kingdom to offer courses in agriculture. In the course of his speech Sir Horace went out of his way to praise the Women's Movement in Ireland and to urge that their example should be followed.

Over the years there were attempts to establish the Women's Institute in England but without success. On 15 June 1915 there was at last a successful launching of the movement in Wales at a meeting in Bangor. There were four prime movers; Mr Nugent Harris, the secretary of the Agriculture Organization Society; Colonel Cotton, Llanfair Pwllgwyngyll; Sir Harry Reichel of UCNW Bangor and Mrs Alfred Watt from Canada who had been campaigning diligently.

Reichel was a strong advocate of the cause of agriculture and rural life. He realized the potential of the movement to set up village halls at the time and was interested in the folk schools of Denmark which had an influence on education in other countries.

Colonel R S G Stapleton-Cotton was an extraordinary man, the son of Viscount Combermere and the nephew of the fourth Marquess of Anglesey. Around 1900, having suffered paralysis of both his legs in South Africa, he came to live at Plas Llwyn Onn, Llanedwen less than 1 mile (1km) from Llanfair. Although he was restricted to a wheelchair he did more for the village than anyone else. He was one of the foremost pioneers of the co-operative movement in North Wales. Not only did he talk; he delivered.

Mrs Watt's address received a warm welcome and the typical response of Colonel Cotton was to convene, the following day, a number of ladies to a meeting in Llanfair.

That was held on 16 June 1915 at a private house, Graig, through the invitation of Mrs W E Jones the wife of the influential estate agent. Colonel Cotton presided and Mrs Watt from British Columbia delivered a lecture. Not only was there warm applause, there was a positive response. It was Mrs Florence Wilson who proposed that a branch of the WI be set up in Llanfair, the first in the United Kingdom. The first meeting was held at Graig and a committee was elected on 11 September 1915. In another meeting on 16 September it was decided to hold subsequent meetings in the Summer House at Graig garden. It was in 1921 that the branch moved to its new home near the tollhouse.

These are some of the topics which were discussed that year; lace-making, poultry and goat keeping, needle work, butter-making and skin-curing, children's welfare and home remedies, chair-repairing and cheese-making. Plenty of variety.

At the first meeting Colonel Cotton read from the Bible and offered a prayer. The men, fair play, expressed the hope that there would be a saner conduct of affairs under the wise influence of women. (This account is based on Dr Constance Bullock Davies's book *A grain of mustard seed).*

THE LAST DAYS OF THE MANSIONS

At the same time as Colonel Cotton of Plas Llwyn Onn was active during the early years of this 20th century two other mansions with their lodges were important establishments. One was Plas Coedmor which Captain Mansell Morgan had built for himself in 1880 and the other was Plas Llanfair which by this time was owned by Mr Harry Clegg.

THE ENGLISH POET AND CRITIC T S ELIOT AND PLAS LLANFAIR

The play *Tom and Viv* by Michael Hastings deals with T S Eliot's first marriage to Vivienne Haigh-Wood. In 1996 a film based on it was released.

In the lengthy introduction and in the text there is a reference to Plas Llanfair. The Haigh-Woods used to go there for a few weeks during the summer months. There is a picture of Vivienne in a greenhouse there in 1914 and there is a facsimile copy of a letter sent by her mother from Plas Llanfair in 1928. Eliot met Vivienne at Oxford in 1914 and they got married in London within six months, so it is possible that Eliot also visited this house.

It was a very unhappy marriage from the beginning and Michael Hastings's research has shown that this unhappy experience had a strong influence on the poem *The Waste Land*. It is interesting to find that Vivienne had a hand in composing lines of some original versions of *The Waste Land.*

Because of her unstable behaviour, partly accounted for by the medication she was being administered, Eliot and her family, probably on the erroneous medical advice given them, arranged for Vivienne to be removed to a mental asylum. She was there for the rest of her days until she died in 1947. The play which was controversial when first produced investigates the tempestuous relationship between these ultra sensitive people and questions the action of the family in ostracizing Vivienne and shows her mother's unease in going ahead with it.

Vivienne was a watercolour artist, a very intelligent and talented young lady and it is probable that some of her poems and short stories may be published in the future.

MR JOHN HORRIDGE AND PLAS LLANFAIR

At the turn of the century Mr Harry Clegg and his family owned and lived in Plas Llanfair. Members of the family have been buried in St Mary's church graveyard, Harry Clegg in 1909.

Later on there is some mystery as to who exactly owned the mansion. There is personal and documentary evidence that a gentleman of the name John Horridge was there between 1919 and 1929 but the Haigh-Wood family used to come there during the same period.

In 1928 Mr Horridge had the first Friezian cow brought to Anglesey. Her name was Melrose Diana. She was killed by lightning in Plas Llanfair farm but fortunately there was a bull calf and a Friezian herd was eventually bred.

THE *INDEFATIGABLE* (1944-1995)

When the Indefatigable, originally a training ship, was closed in the summer of 1995 the name was Indefatigable School. It was an independent school for boys with an up-to-date course of study in line with National Curriculum recommendations and an emphasis on outdoor activities. The boys wore the usual ratings uniform, rehearsed regularly for the band and learned parade-ground skills. In 1994 the school celebrated 50 years at Plas Llanfair on the edge of the Menai Straits, bought from the Marquess of Anglesey.

In January 1865 the frigate HMS *Indefatigable* which had been launched at Devonport in 1848, was loaned to Merseyside, towed to Liverpool and was then called the *Indefatigable* Training Ship. She was moored off New Ferry along with HMS *Conway* and other old-fashioned wooden ships.

In 1912 she was replaced by HMS *Phaeton* which was bought from the Admiralty for £5,000 donated by James Bibby. She was a steel-built cruiser fully rigged for sail. A sister ship to *Arethusa, Ampheon* and *Leander*, she was launched in Glasgow in 1883. In 1914 she was taken to her moorings at Rock Ferry and renamed *Indefatigable*, the first steel vessel to be used as a training ship for boys.

From 1914 until the Second World War she prepared a large number of boys for naval careers. She was refitted in 1941 and was in Glasgow as a store ship and for training merchant seamen gunners during the war. She was broken up in 1947.

Because of the bombing of Liverpool in the early part of the Second World War the school was moved to Clawdd Newydd near Rhuthun at a disused boys' holiday camp. It was established at Plas Llanfair in 1944.

THE *CLIO*

Between 1877 and 1920 the most prominent feature on the Menai Straits was the *Clio*, the industrial training ship moored at Garth ferry opposite Bangor pier.

Although it was customary to threaten naughty boys and truants with being sent to the *Clio*, the ship was not a Reformatory School. An Industrial Training School fulfilled two purposes; to provide lodging, food and clothing for homeless, destitute and poor boys and to provide future seamen.

The *Clio* was a 200 ton corvette with three masts and engines. Built of oak, she was launched in 1858 and looked like HMS *Conway*.

HMS *CONWAY*

During the Second World War the *Conway* was moved from the Mersey to the Menai Straits to where the *Clio* had been. She was moved again in 1948 to moorings near Plas Newydd. She was designed as a training college for officers mostly the sons of professional men.

YNYS GORAD GOCH (THE ISLAND BETWEEN THE TWO BRIDGES)

One of the finest views in Anglesey is that from the lay-by on the bottom road from Llanfair to Menai Bridge. From here the two bridges can be clearly seen as well as the Straits and the Arfon mountains in the background. It is beautiful in the blue and green of Summer, dramatic when there is a high tide and very attractive when there is snow on the mountains. But one feature is not appreciated during the daytime, the floodlit Menai Suspension Bridge against a dark background at night. There is a pavement on one side of the road making it a pleasant walk and there are convenient lay-bys for those visiting in a coach or car.

Roughly half way between the bridges, in the middle of the Straits lies Ynys Gorad Goch with its one house and outbuildings. In 1590 it was referred to as Ynys Madog Goch (The Island of Madog the Red) and it is thought that it was thus called after a Bishop of Bangor who lived in the 14th century.

Cored is the Welsh word for weir, a device for trapping fish on beaches and in rivers by means of wattle fencing. The principle is simple. At low tide the weir, about 6ft (1.8m) high, is exposed. After coming in with the rising tide some fish continue swimming and feeding inside the weir and ultimately find that the means of escape has disappeared as the tide goes out. The method was being used by stone age man about 3,000 BC or earlier.

The position of the island which is in two halves, with the Cribiniau rocks on the Arfon side, is in the middle of the Straits. There are two weirs, the one on the Anglesey side larger than the other. On close inspection we see today stone walls about a yard wide reinforced with concrete built on to the rocks. They form reservoirs at high tide but there are large holes with grids to let the water out as the tide recedes. The weirs are in a state of disrepair. Traditionally there were wattle fences on top of dry stone walls with plenty of nooks and crevices to harbour marine life and to allow small fish to enter the weir. These are some of the species of fish caught in the weir; herring, whiting, cod, bass, pollock and flatfish; whitebait were sometimes plentiful so that white bait teas used to be served. Gorad Goch was sometimes called 'White Bait Island'.

At the beginning of the 20th century one well known occupier was Mr Madog Jones and his family. They would come regularly to chapel three times on Sunday using a rowing boat to cross the fifty yards to the shore.

Once after a gale Madog Jones found that one boat was missing. After many enquiries it was found, beached at Moelfre. Without hesitation Madog picked up a couple of oars, walked across a part of Anglesey and rowed the boat round Black Point, Penmon and up the Straits home. His grand-daughter would confidently row herself to Menai Bridge or Caernarfon. She lived to the good age of ninety two.

PWLLFANOG

Pwllfanog is strictly in the parish of Llanedwen but as it is so near it has always been regarded as a part of Llanfair. In documents going back to the 16th century the name of the little harbour and village was Aber Pwllfanogl. It was a busy small port with thriving industries at the beginning of the 20th century. At that time the road to Plas Newydd and the lane to Pwllfanog would be very busy with men and boys, women and girls going to and from work at the harbour, the factories on the site and at the mansion, its farm and gardens.

Being in a very sheltered position, Pwllfanog was an ideal harbour and it has another advantage, the water power from the swiftly descending River Braint. Around the middle of the 19th century the mill pool extended over a wide area south of the station. A map dated 1841, that is before building the railway, shows it reaching as far as the site of the James Pringle shop towards a smallholding known as Glan Llyn (Lake Side). From this lake the water rushed down through Aber Braint, taking in the water from the River Rhyd Eilian which goes through Llanfair, to Plas Newydd park. There was a reservoir about half a mile up the valley from Pwllfanog from which there was a channel guiding the water to drive the large wheel of the slate works on the west side of Pwllfanog. Part of the river was used to power the flour mill. Before the end of the 19th century there had been a gas works but a proposal by Menai Bridge Supply Co Ltd to produce electricity did not materialize.

Compared with its present state the site extended further down the foreshore with two sea walls projecting to form a quay facing the Straits as well as the one on the river bank.

There is a reference to the flour mill in the 16th century. The main industry was the production of school writing slates but sailing ships and, later, steam ships brought in coal as well as the raw material, slate. The slate works employed as many as forty men and boys, the men in 1898 being paid ten shillings for a six-day week, from 7.30am to 6.30pm and the boys nine pence a week. Sand was brought in from Traeth Lafan and early in the 19th century there was a lime kiln. A plan shows a cook-shop where the workers could get refreshments and a pub, the 'Pilot Boat'. Later there were factories making margarine, curing bacon and drying and grinding chicory, these being some of Colonel Cotton's enterprises. He was also behind the setting up of an egg-packing depot at the railway station site, a bulb-growing project in the field opposite Llwyn as well as poultry-keeping and gardening. All this activity necessitated considerable traffic on the lane to Pwllfanog, mainly horse-drawn vehicles, as its heyday as an industrial village had passed before the advent of the motor car. Until about 1950 the pool in the estuary was the one place where the village children enjoyed themselves diving and swimming, but now it is quiet apart from the few fishermen who have traditionally kept their boats on the beach.

SHIPS

Two fairly large ships which called at Pwllfanog to export writing slates were the steamers *Ibis* and *Christiana* with the Welshman Captain Griffith as master. The *Ibis* sank in 1895 after only two years' service. The *Christiana* was operating between 1901 and 1920; she was 130ft (39.6m) long and had been built in Paisley on the Clyde. Earlier the *King Ja Ja* (1874-1891), an iron ship built in Glasgow and her successor the *Prince Ja Ja* (1890-1902) were often mentioned in connection with Pwllfanog. Both were named after the King of Opobio in Nigeria, the *Prince* being built by William Thomas at Amlwch, Anglesey. The trade consisted of groceries from Morris and Jones and David Jones, Liverpool and general cargo for Caernarfon, Y Felinheli, Porthaethwy, Bangor, and Beaumaris. It was possible to carry roofing slates on the return voyage from Porth Penrhyn, Y Felinheli and Caernarfon as well as writing slates from Pwllfanog.

The above-mentioned Captain Griffith, in a letter published in his Welsh book *Yr Hen Forwr* (The Old Sailor), says that he had taken writing slates to a number of foreign countries from Pwllfanog. He records that, many years earlier when men were excavating for foundations for a building, they came across vaults that no one knew about. His opinion was that they had been hiding places by smugglers bringing in spirits and tobacco.

It is claimed that at least one ship was built at Pwllfanog. Many seafaring families lived there including Captain Peter Jones, one of seven brothers who all went to sea having started on sailing ships.

Other ships mentioned by older residents include, the *Dusty Miller, Harlow Plain, Roma* and *Mary B Mitchell.* At the beginning of this century, four steamers belonging to the Dinorwig (Llanberis) quarries were working in the Straits; *Elidir, Dinorwig, Enid* and *Velinheli (sic).*

The ships used to pick up the pilot not far from Plas Newydd to guide them through the dangerous channels and currents between the two bridges and put him down at Menai Bridge pier.

THE ROMAN INVASION OF ANGLESEY 61 AD

Opposite Y Felinheli lies the remaining part of the jetty that served the Moel y Don ferry. It is about 3 miles (4.8km) from Llanfair down a lane towards the Straits from the Brynsiencyn, Newborough main road. Along this lane on the right stands Plas Coch, a fine Elizabethan style mansion built of red sandstone where there is today a caravan park and where the popular Anglesey Steam Rally is held annually in May attracting many thousands to the two day event. During the summer very popular car boot sales are held here on Sundays and a large one is held throughout the year at the Anglesey Show field.

From this tranquil spot on the edge of the Straits the Moel y Don ferry across to Y Felinheli ran until the middle of this century. Before the days of the motor car it was a very convenient short cut to the mainland rather than going all the way to the Menai Bridge. Anglesey men who worked in Llanberis quarry crossed here and were able to ride on the quarry train from Y Felinheli to their place of work.

It was probably near here that Ynys Môn first leapt dramatically on to the stage of history in 61 AD. That was the time of the first invasion of Anglesey by the **Romans** and the first time for **Mona** to appear in a document, in the work of the Roman historian Tacitus.

Although Tacitus does not refer specifically to this particular spot it is the most likely crossing place. Henry Rowlands in *Mona Antiqua* quoted a place-name Pant yr Ysgraphie (the Lowland of the Barges) in support of this claim. Abermenai, south east of Newborough has also been suggested. Another possible crossing place that has been suggested is from Traeth Lafan to Beaumaris but that would have meant carrying heavy equipment over miles of sand. And, further, the description by Tacitus is notable for the detail of what could be seen and heard. That suggests a setting where the Straits are narrow and the opposite shore quite near. The general Suetonius Paulinus who was a first rate soldier had planned carefully and had barges prepared for the landing.

The historian's description is famous. Wild-looking women wearing black and with their hair dishevelled were weaving in and out amongst the Anglesey warriors, carrying torches and screaming and gesticulating in a most threatening manner. At the same time the white-robed druids with arms upraised were uttering awful curses in loud voices. The whole scene was so terrible that the Roman soldiers were mesmerized. But when urged on by their commanders they took courage and went on to defeat the Celts and then they proceeded to kill the druids and destroy their sanctuaries. Although Tacitus was writing as a Roman, not a neutral observer, the account is extremely valuable.

Mona was undoubtedly the last home of the Druids. It is possible that some of them had fled here from Southern Britain and Gaul before the Roman armies. Julius Caesar wrote that that they had originally come from Britain before some had gone to Gaul and that it was to Britain that disciples were sent to be trained in the secret traditions. All this was done orally and took many years to complete.Being themselves members of the aristocracy, the druids held the highest positions in society. They were the leaders who could communicate with the gods and the other world by creating the correct atmosphere, conducting ceremonies and sacrifices and prophesying through the interpretation of signs from the entrails of slain animals and humans. There is evidence that they were skilful astronomers. And yet they remain mysterious priests because their secrets had to be guarded most carefully. They were the religious leaders of the Celts before and during the Roman occupation of Britain. They may well have survived into Christian times. J Markale in *Celtic Civilization* claims that the druids survived in Ireland until the 10th century. There is agreement that Anglesey with its oak groves was an important centre for the druids. Perhaps that is why it is sometimes called the Dark Island.

A short period after the first attack on Anglesey Suetonius was recalled to the south east of Britain to put down a revolt by the *Iceni* under their leader Buddug or *Boudicea*. But by the year 84 AD Julius Agricola had advanced from Deva or Chester and taken the island completing the conquest of Wales.

AFON BRAINT

The river that runs through Llanfair between Siglen and Sarn Faban and under the main road near the new cemetery is Rhyd Eilian. It runs into the larger River

Braint which, coming past Tyddyn y Felin and Pandy, goes under the main road west of Bryngof. Near Star at Rhos Bothan it forks, one part flowing towards Dwyran and the other back to Llanfair through Aber Braint to Pwllfanog.

Braint is a very old name. Sir Ifor Williams explained it in *Enwau Lleoedd* as a name derived from the Brythonic name of the goddess Brigantia and related to the Welsh word 'braint' (privilege); so she was the queen, the most privileged person in society. There was an important Celtic tribe in the north of Britain called *Brigantes*. The river was held in high esteem as a goddess and as a manifestation of her magical power and mystique. In Irish literature the name of the goddess was Brigit and she was later adopted as the Christian St Brigid. She was an important goddess worshipped by the Celts generally and was associated with the second of the main Celtic pagan feasts on February the first. Their first one was Samain, November the first, when there used to be great celebrations. They believed that the veil between the other world and this one was very thin at this particular time, that the dead arose and that ghosts and witches were abroad. The Church changed it to 'All Saints Feast'.

THE HEN DŶ STONE HEAD

It was not until 1970 when *Prehistoric Anglesey* by Frances Lynch was published that this Celtic stone head that used to be on a wall outside the farmhouse Hen Dŷ, Llanfair Pwllgwyngyll became widely known. The farm gate is roughly half way between St Tysilio nursing home and the Four Crosses pub on the top road from Llanfair to Menai Bridge. It was probably carved during the time of the Celts of the Iron Age around 500 BC from red sandstone. More recently other stone heads have come to light at Llanallgo and Llangeinwen. A large number of heads in stone and wood have been found in Britain, Ireland and other European countries. They are discussed in full with illustrations By Dr Anne Ross in *Pagan Celtic Britain.*

The Hen Dŷ head probably represented a Celtic god and the slightly concave flat top of the head was probably used for placing offerings. In fact the claim has recently been made that this specific rite has been observed throughout the ages until this century by votaries of the old religion of the Celts.

These carved heads may well be a manifestation of the cult of the head by the Celts. It is established that it was their custom to cut off the head of the defeated enemy, carry it off on the horse's saddle and have it preserved as a trophy. It seems that this was more than barbarous bravado, that in fact it signified their belief in the particular power of the human head.

The story of Branwen daughter of Llŷr, the sea-god of British mythology, in the Welsh tales, the *Mabinogion* relates that after the bitter fighting in Ireland only seven of the men of Britain and Branwen remained alive. The leader, Bendigeidfran, had been mortally wounded and he commanded them to cut off his head and carry it with them home. When they reached Anglesey Branwen died but the seven men went on to Harlech and Pembroke and under the mysterious influence of the head they lived for many years in a blessed state of happiness. When he led his men to battle Bendigeidfran had stretched over a river forming a bridge over which his soldiers could cross. He was superhuman and his head, after decapitation, had the power of a god. Time stood still and in his presence the survivors seemed to be in paradise.

The Hen Dŷ head was removed to Oriel Môn early in the 1990's.

CRAIG Y DINAS LLANFAIR PWLLGWYNGYLL - HILL-FORTS

The rocky hill on which the Marquess of Anglesey's column stands is called Craig y Dinas, 'craig' meaning 'rock' and 'dinas' although corresponding to 'city' today formerly meant 'fort'. During the centuries before the birth of Christ and for some time afterwards this high point with a commanding view of the Straits probably served as a small hill-fort for Celtic and pre-Celtic tribes.

The first part of 'dinas', 'din', is found in the names of Welsh hill-forts such as Dinorben and Dinmor in Penmon. The cognate is found in Dun Laoghaire in Ireland, Dundee in Scotland and Dunkerque in France. There are a large number in Caernarfonshire, Pen y Gaer above Tal-y-Cafn in the Conwy valley, Craig y Dinas in Dyffryn Nantlle, Dinas Emrys near Beddgelert, Braich y Dinas on the summit of Penmaen-mawr (near Graig Lwyd the famous source of stone axes in the Neolithic Age), which has been completely destroyed by quarrying and the outstanding example at Tre'r Ceiri, between Clynnog and Nefyn, one of the most remarkable in Britain, covering five acres with the perimeter wall still standing, about 4.5yds (4m) high in places. Within there are the remaining walls of a hundred and fifty round huts all dating from about 200 BC and situated 1,312ft (400m) above sea level. Dinas Dinorwig in the parish of Llanddeiniolen, a hill-fort covering about three acres, has the distinction of retaining the name of the important tribe, the Ordovicians.

DINSYLWY OR ARTHUR'S TABLE

Three of the hill-forts on Anglesey are situated very near the coast facing North; Caer y Twr covering about 17 acres on Holyhead Mountain, Dinas Gynfor near

Cemaes (about 24 acres) and Llanfihangel Dinsylwy or Arthur's Table the best known, near Llanddona about 8 miles (13km) from Llanfair. It has been suggested that Sylwy is derived from *Selgovae,* a tribe that gave its name to Solway in Scotland with the implication that there had been early immigration from the north. It is worth a visit to appreciate the splendid scenery over land and sea. On the way from Llanddona to Glanrafon and Llangoed above Red Wharf Bay there is a tall television mast on the left. A short distance down a hill there is a stile from which it is about ten minutes' walk to the hill-fort covering an area of 17 acres. Taking advantage of the site high above the Irish sea and with rock outcrops forming low cliffs in places it is ideal as a watching post and a defensive retreat. The main protective wall consists of two rows of very large limestone boulders on edge running parallel, while the middle is filled in with earth and rubble.

There has not been any serious archaeological digging to ascertain the date of its building but studies of similar hill-forts suggest a date c. 1,000 BC. It was probably in full use also some centuries before the birth of Christ and during the Roman occupation up to c. 400 AD. The prefix *din* is also found in the names of much more compact walled enclosures such as the fascinating **Din Llugwy** west of Moelfre containing the remains of houses or possibly a palace from the 4th century AD. It has walls of large slabs of limestone, similar to those at Dinsylwy, forming a compact set of buildings that is, in its fine condition, unique in Wales. The Llugwy burial chamber, not far away, has a massive 28 ton capstone.

BRONZE AGE

Waves of different people came to Britain from the Continent over the centuries. The discovery in the Middle East of bronze, an alloy of copper and tin spread to Europe. The theory is that bronze manufacturers from Europe exported artefacts and weapons of this useful metal to Britain from around 2,500 BC and that some bronze-workers came here to follow their trade. It seems that a sufficient number of invaders of this age came here so as to be able to impose their will on the indigenous population. Din Sylwy with its enclosure of 17 acres would have been a safe retreat for families and their livestock for a period. Considering the size of the fort and the gigantic task of building it one concludes that there must have been a powerful ruler supported by a military force to organize and enforce the building operations. This does not preclude the possibility that influential chieftains of the native tribes were able to arrange for their own people to master the new technology and that they themselves co-operated with the newcomers.

THE IRON AGE

From about 500 BC it is fairly certain that people speaking a Celtic language came here. They were warlike tribes having weapons of iron and able to utilize chariots with iron-tyred wheels drawn by small horses.

During the period under consideration the language that was spoken over most of Britain was the British form of Celtic or Brythonic which, during the 4th and 5th centuries AD developed into Welsh. It was a language similar to Latin with its declensions and conjugations and very similar to the Celtic language of Gaul where there was, for example, a place-name *Uindomagos* written *Uindomagus* by the Romans. There would have been an equivalent word in Brythonic, the spoken word *uindo* changing over the years to give the Welsh 'gwyn' while the *magos* developed into 'ma' and then 'fa' thus explaining the derivation of the Welsh word 'gwynfa' (paradise). Many place-names in England as well as Scotland are derived from British Celtic. Here are some examples; Aberdeen (aber: estuary), Stratford upon Avon (afon: river), Crewe (cryw: fish weir), Lanark (llannerch: glade, clear space), London (Londonion; Latin Londonium), Penrith (pen: end, rhyd < *ritu*: ford).

This British Celtic language of the Iron Age people was that of the upper classes of society, the warring kings, the druids, the poets and the lawyers. It had been so well-established amongst them that it was able to withstand Latin, the official language of the Roman Empire over four centuries of occupation and develop into a new language, Cymraeg (Welsh).

TALL FAIR PEOPLE

These people who are called Celts because of their language were tall and strong with a fair complexion, the women being as strong and brave as the men. The chief soldiers wore a colourful tunic, trousers and a cloak with a brooch on the shoulder and a gold torque around the neck. The main weapons were the long sword and the spear and they took particular delight in their decorated shields. The speed at which they could drive their chariots and keep their balance to throw their spears was remarkable.

By taking advantage of metals and the iron-tyred wheel they were able to advance agriculture and raise living standards. Some became very wealthy taking great pride in their gold possessions and class distinction was evident amongst them. At the top was the king and his army, then the priesthood consisting of the druids, the poets and seers, the lawyers, doctors, musicians and craftsmen. The manual workers on land and sea were slaves. The artefacts that have been recovered, to be seen in museums, show clearly that their metal workers had attained a high standard of craftsmanship and artistry in iron, bronze and gold.

In the series *Shire Archaeology* there is an attractive book *Celtic Warriors* by W F and J N G Ritchie containing interesting pictures and references to scholarly books. Another relevant book in the same series is *Hill-Forts of England and Wales.*

BRONZE AND IRON AGE FINDS

It was reported in *Archaeologia Cambrensis* 1856 that two bronze axes or celts were discovered while ploughing a field in Rhos y Gath, Llanfair. The larger was in excellent condition and the other one which was smaller was Irish. Both have been lost but there is a picture of the Irish celt. Not far from the Anglesey end of the Suspension Bridge a collection of eight such bronze celts were found; one is in the museum in Bangor, one in Cardiff and one in the British Museum. A bronze pin, as mentioned earlier, was found in the graveyard of Llanfair church early in the 20th century.

One of the most important Iron Age discoveries in Britain was made near Valley, Anglesey in 1943, the Llyn Cerrig Bach hoard, including swords, spears, shields, the remains of chariots and harnesses, slave-gang chains, trumpets, cauldrons and other vessels made of bronze and iron, excellent examples of the La Tene culture. They can be seen at Oriel Môn and the National Museum, Cardiff.

OLDER ARCHAEOLOGICAL FINDS

The oldest finds are stone axes and hammers from the **New Stone Age**, that is from around 4,000 BC or earlier. The earliest type were roughly shaped stones strapped on to a socketed haft, followed by an edged and polished implement and ultimately pierced stones of high quality fitting over a wooden shaft. Unpierced stone tools have been found in Penmynydd, Llansadwrn, Gaerwen, Pentraeth, Plas Newydd and other places. An axe made of the Craig y Dinas, Llanfair, stone was found in Llandrillo yn Rhos while two hammers and a stone mortar were found near Craig y Dinas. One hammer is in the National Museum in Cardiff and the other is in the museum in Bangor. They are described technically as a mining tool used in the Bronze Age between 2,000 and 1,000 BC the original period of mining copper at Mynydd Parys near Amlwch, and the Great Orme near Llandudno.

Fairly recently two stone axes were found at Pwllfanog one which was found in the water by Mr Terence Greenham and the other reported by Mr J Kyffin Williams as being in private ownership in Cardiff. Many stone tools are from the famous Graig Lwyd, Penmaen-mawr and a number of them are pierced.

The evidence remaining from the Neolithic dolmens consist of such stone implements and weapons and pieces of pottery. At Graig Lwyd, Penmaen-mawr craftsmen were able to chip stones into the rough shape and size. At Llandygai and Bryn yr Hen Bobl near Plas Newydd evidence has been found that these were centres for polishing and sharpening these stones for local use and for export to distant places. At the tip of the **Llŷn** peninsula there was a stone axe factory similar to Graig Lwyd but on a smaller scale at Mynydd Rhiw.

The Neolithic people continued to use flint as well, as it was such useful material and as John Davies reminds us, every age was the age of wood. Wood was vitally important for tool shafts, for posts, gates, doors and so on. In the round or square houses of wood or part-stone whose roofs of turf or thatch had a wooden frame, they had utensils and furniture of wood and leather. They could spin wool and weave cloth on a simple weaving frame. These New Stone Age invaders from Europe brought farming to Wales. With their improved implements they were able to cut down trees and make clearings. At first they fitted the axe through a socket in the wooden shaft and strengthened the joint with leather thong. Later they were able to make a socket in the axe by rotating a hard sharp-pointed stone to drill a hole with the aid of sand. In recent experiments it has been shown that these primitive axes were extremely efficient for cutting down trees. These farmers made hay, grew crops of grain and flax from which they could make string, ropes, nets and a hessian type fabric. They had cattle, sheep, goats and pigs and the dog had been trained to be a faithful friend.

People of the **Old Stone Age** were clever enough to have made effective scrapers, knives, spears and arrow heads from sharp-edged **flint** stones. They had shown ingenuity in using wood and antler horns to make tools and had mastered the craft of making nets, traps and snares to catch animals, birds and fish. There is no direct evidence of these from our area of North Wales but on the basis of materials preserved in peat in other places it is reasonable to assume that they were used here also. These people are usually described as hunters and gatherers.

The Cromlech or Neolithic people, then, had inherited the equipment and the clever hunting and fishing methods of their ancestors and had developed into semi-nomadic farmers. They had perfected many techniques which show intelligence, organization and perseverance.

THE DOLMEN OR CROMLECH AT TŶ MAWR

On the top road from Llanfair to Menai Bridge, in the second field on the left after the bridge over the by-pass remain the large stones of a cromlech or passage grave.

The huge capstone weighing about 10 tons has slipped from the three large blue stones which have partly collapsed. The capstone measures about 11ft by 8ft (3.35m by 2.4m) while an old map shows a cairn about 49ft by 32ft (15m by 10m). The Rev Hugh Pritchard in *Archaeologia Cambrensis* 1873 wrote that he had heard it said that hut foundations had been removed from the field that lies below the rock behind the cromlech. Tŷ Mawr is one of a group of three similar early megaliths in Anglesey the other two being Bodowyr near Brynsiencyn and Tŷ Newydd near Rhosneigr. Tŷ Mawr has not been the subject of an archaeological dig but by comparing it with two similar megaliths in Anglesey and others in South Wales, Ireland, Devon, Brittany and Spain it is thought that it was built about 3,500 BC. It is maintained that the sea, at this early period, was the connecting link between people of different countries. The background and significance are discussed in detail by Frances Lynch in *Prehistoric Anglesey.* John Davies in his history of Wales notes that the dolmens belong to the far Western parts of Europe and that they are the first permanent structures built by man. He makes the point that the oldest of them are nearly 1,500 years older than the oldest of the Pyramids of Egypt. Stonehenge was built between 2,800 and 1,400 BC. Tŷ Mawr is one of the oldest megaliths in Anglesey from about 3,500 BC.

A BURIAL PLACE

In essence a dolmen was the grave of a clan over many years. It may be that the bodies were first buried at another place and that the bones were ultimately brought together and at some stage the tomb was covered over with earth and stones. But it was more than a grave; it was hallowed ground. It was at this spot, probably, that these ancient people held ceremonies, revered relics, uttered the mystical words of their religion, sought the gods' blessing on their crops and livestock and celebrated the changing of the seasons in song and dance. By showing due reverence to the memory of their ancestors they were also stating their right to the land.

BRYN CELLI DDU (THE MOUND OF THE DARK GROVE)

This is a well-known passage grave in the parish of Llanddaniel-fab. From Llanfair the simplest way is to take the Newborough road at the tollhouse and having passed Plas Newydd take the first right turn to Llanedwen school where there is a prominent ancient monument sign. The key is obtainable at the farm near the burial chamber. A detailed archaeological description and references to research work can be found in Frances Lynch's *Prehistoric Anglesey.*

This cromlech has been restored, is widely known and attracts visitors from far afield to see it. It is one of the latest burial chambers built about 2,500 to 2,000 BC being noteworthy not only because of the central chamber containing a circular stone column 5ft 6ins (1.6m) above floor level, but also because it has been built on the site of an earlier circular religious centre. These are called 'henges' which

Tŷ Mawr Cromlech *Photo Emyr Pritchard*

Bryn Celli Ddu *Photo Derec Owen*

Hen Dŷ Head *Photo Derec Owen*

served also as meeting places for ceremonial purposes and probably for trading. The significance of Bryn Celli Ddu is that the remains show a conflict of two sets of people with differing religious traditions. Around 3,000 to 2,500 BC newcomers to the area built the henge but later people who disapproved and who still kept their allegiance to former religious traditions came and destroyed the henge. They then built their ancient style burial chamber on the site. A marked feature of this burial chamber is the passage made of upright stones leading to the central chamber.

Barclodiad y Gawres burial chamber above Porth Trecastell, near Aberffraw from about 2,500 BC is similar to tombs such as Newgrange in Ireland. Described by Frances Lynch as 'one of the finest and most interesting of all the North Welsh tombs', Barclodiad y Gawres is remarkable for the abstract designs on carved stones not found anywhere else in mainland Britain.

SIR JOHN MORRIS-JONES OF LLANFAIR PWLLGWYNGYLL

Sir John Morris-Jones (1864-1929) was the first Professor of Welsh at the University College of North Wales, Bangor, the author of *A Welsh Grammar* (1913) and *Cerdd Dafod* (1925) an authoritative work on Welsh poetry from medieval times. He was also a fine poet and critic who had a lasting effect on Welsh poetry and the literary language. He translated the *Rubaiyat* of Omar Khayyam into Welsh. Appreciating the contribution made by Lewis Morris and Goronwy Owen's circle in the 18th century John Morris-Jones was determined that the initiative for another literary revival would come from Anglesey.

Sir John played a major role in creating the conditions for a remarkable renaissance in both poetry and prose in the Welsh language. To some extent credit should go to his students who graduated and became teachers in the colleges and secondary schools. He and his followers were able to engender admiration and enthusiasm for the Welsh literature of former times, including the medieval period, which in its turn inspired scholars to research and writers to write for their own age in a contemporary idiom. His successors in the chair of Welsh at Bangor, Sir Ifor Williams, Sir Thomas Parry, Professor J E Caerwyn Williams and others have maintained the high standard of scholarship. Of course, there have been brilliant contributions in research and scholarship by members of other departments of the University College.

Sir John was not the only influence on literature. For example, Eifion Wyn from Porthmadog wrote fine lyrical poems in the tradition of Ceiriog, one of the best known being a poem about Cwm Pennant, the winding valley of the Dwyfor behind Garndolbenmaen. Also the great hymns of the 18th and 19th centuries were well known and provided a pattern in form and language. The name of the shepherd poet Hedd Wyn is well known because of the tragic circumstances in 1917 when he won the National Eisteddfod chair at Birkenhead for his poem *Yr Arwr* (The Hero) but had been killed at Pilkem Ridge in Belgium a few weeks earlier. The film about his life made a few years ago is one of the best in the Welsh language and in 1994 was the first Welsh language film to be nominated for a Hollywood Oscar. The bronze memorial statue on a granite base at Trawsfynydd by L S Merrifield (1923) is a dramatic representation of the poet. The outstanding poets from the area covered in this book were W J Gruffydd, R Williams Parry, T H Parry-Williams, Cynan, Caradog Pritchard and Gwilym R Jones. W J Gruffydd, T H Parry-Williams and Caradog Pritchard excelled in prose as well. The three and Kate Roberts, T Rowland Hughes and John Gwilym Jones were prose writers from the slate quarrying areas. The family of the most distinguished scholar and literary figure J Saunders Lewis, from the mother's side, came from Anglesey and Caernarfonshire. The quality of writing was maintained by succeeding generations and excellent work is still being produced. It was fine scholarship and splendid works of literature which were the most significant contribution of Gwynedd to the life of Wales in the first half of the 20th century.

THE RED HOUSE

The most famous house in the village is Tŷ Coch, the house built for Sir John Morris-Jones in the centre of Llanfair. While he was at Oxford John Morris-Jones came under the influence of the teachings of John Ruskin (1819-1900) and William Morris (1834-1896). Ruskin taught his generation to appreciate Gothic architecture and in admirable prose taught people to admire the paintings of the Pre-Raphaelites and J M W Turner. William Morris read his *Modern Painters* and *The Stones of Venice* with enthusiasm and *The Nature of Gothic* was as a bible for him. Examples of the Gothic style are Westminster Abbey and the cathedrals of Chartres and Notre Dame. During the 19th century, under the influence of Ruskin and others, there was renewed interest in Gothic architecture and many churches were built or refurbished in the neo-Gothic fashion as well as some secular buildings such as Manchester Town Hall.

William Morris looked back in admiration at the craft-work of the Middle Ages. He built a house for himself and his wife Jane (née Burden) in the village of Upton in Kent. He rejected the square box-type contemporary dwellings with slate roofs and rendered walls and decided on an L-shaped house of red brick with a high-pitched roof of red tiles. In the process of designing this house and its furnishings William Morris started a revolution in domestic architecture, furniture and fabrics. He called their new home The Red House.

Although the house in Llanfair is of red brick and tiles unlike most houses in the vicinity the resemblance to William Morris's house is not marked. However it is L-shaped and inside, the inglenook and oak panelling are reminiscent of Morris.

THE YOUNG WALES MOVEMENT - CYMDEITHAS 'CYMRU FYDD'

The last decades of the 19th century was a very exciting time in Welsh politics and some important aspirations were realized. The County Councils were established after 1888 and the Welsh Intermediate Education Act was passed in 1889. The influential institutions of primary and secondary education, colleges and a university (1893) were established and the National Library and Museum in the first decade of the new century. A group of young men played a role in this renaissance, building on the achievements of earlier campaigners such as Hugh Owen in the field of education. In 1886 a small group of young men in Oxford University met and founded a Welsh society, Cymdeithas Dafydd ap Gwilym named after the outstanding poet from the 14th century. Apart from the far-reaching achievements of individual members in the social and literary fields in later life, they allied themselves as young Liberals with such able and energetic politicians as Tom Ellis and Lloyd George. Tom Ellis who was the founder of 'Cymru Fydd' (Young Wales) in London in 1886 was greatly influenced by Ireland. The Irish *Sinn Fein* means 'ourselves'. It implies that it is upon the courage, self sacrifice, unity and exertions of the Irish people themselves that the future of the Irish nation depends. The basis of the policy is national self reliance. John Hugh Edwards in his *Life of Lloyd George* quotes from a speech by Tom Ellis: 'Some are overwhelmed by the apparent hopelessness of Wales. They seem to scorn the possibilities of a distinct regeneration of Wales. ... The elements of regeneration have been fermenting for a century. A yearning for better things is the heart's desire of the masses and youth of Wales at the present day. Her great need is the moral leverage of reform. Foremost is the consciousness of distinct nationality'.

The main political issues were land reform, disestablishment of the church and home rule. The movement spread from London and Oxford and under the influence of John Morris-Jones the first branch in Wales was set up in Llanfair Pwllgwyngyll in 1887. The minutes of the meetings, kept at the archives, University of Wales, Bangor provide an insight into the social and political life of one village and of Wales. The views expressed were very radical and it is interesting that John Morris-Jones, a Liberal, was invited to stand as a parliamentary candidate for the Socialists in Anglesey in 1887. While the Young Wales Society contained a strong cultural element, Lloyd George and others formed a more political Cymru Fydd League in 1894 with the emphasis on self-government. It collapsed in 1896.

Also reflecting the wider Welsh national Non-conformist scene was the fact that the life of the community turned round the chapels of the Calvinistic Methodists, the Wesleyans and the Congregationalists, the nearest Baptist chapel being about 2 miles (3.2km) from Llanfair. There were two services as well as Sunday school for adults and children on Sunday together with supplementary meetings, and prayer and other meetings on most evenings during the week. The most dramatic event before the Great War was a religious revival throughout Wales under the influence of Evan Roberts in 1904-5.

RADICAL LIBERALS

The Liberal Thomas Edward Ellis (1859-1899) was elected for Meirioneth in 1886 and David Lloyd George (1863-1945) joined him in 1890. These two politicians and the historian and campaigner O M Edwards were greatly influenced by Michael D Jones (1822-98) a Congregationalist minister from Bala. His mother had been evicted because he had refused to support their landlord Sir Watcyn Williams Wynn. The two years 1848-1850 which he spent as the minister of the Welsh chapel at Cincinnati in the United States confirmed him in his nationalist principles. He was one of the leaders of the movement to establish a Welsh colony in Patagonia. This is a statement which he made in 1856: ‘Because the Welsh are oppressed in their own country ... they have lost their self confidence; they do not believe that they can achieve much with the result that they attempt little. They believe, as all slaves do, that only the master has the ability ...’. The Irish liberation movement and national leaders like Mazzini in Italy influenced his young followers.

The pressure within the Liberal party for home rule became so strong that Lord Rosebery, then Prime Minister, in 1895 came out strongly in favour of self government for Wales on the same lines as proposals for Ireland and Scotland. A few months later the House of Commons decided ‘that this house is of the opinion ... that it would be appropriate to transfer to legislatures in Ireland, Scotland, Wales and England, the control and government of their domestic affairs’.

Between 1910 and 1914 E T John who became the Liberal member for East Denbighshire campaigned vigorously and introduced a Self Government measure in the House of Commons in 1914. Disillusioned, he later joined the Labour Party.

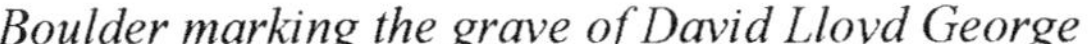
Boulder marking the grave of David Lloyd George

‘THE BIG STICK IS THE LITTLE PENCIL IN THE VOTING BOOTH’

David Lloyd George
National Library of Wales

Tom Ellis
National Library of Wales

O M Edwards
National Library of Wales

John Morris-Jones
Photo Miss Nest Morris-Jones

Photograph taken outside Professors' corridor UCNW Bangor on the occasion of the National Eisteddfod at Bangor 1915.

Left to right: Nest Morris-Jones, Megan, David and Mrs Lloyd George, Gwenllïan, Rhiannon, Mrs John Morris-Jones, Angharad and John Morris-Jones, Sir Vincent Evans. Behind Lloyd George, Sir John Prichard-Jones (Patron of Prichard-Jones Hall Bangor and Institute, Newborough), Mrs Nancy Morris, Llywelyn Williams MP for Carmarthen Boroughs, J Evan Morris (Morris & Jones Liverpool). Behind John Morris-Jones and left Thomas Shankland Librarian.

Photo Miss Nest Morris-Jones.

Pwllheli: Abererch Bay to the right of marina, old town centre inland from marina. Snowdon and Moel Hebog to right in background.
Photo and sponsored by Dŵr Cymru / Welsh Water.

Snowdon Mountain Railway, Glaslyn (near) and Llyn Llydaw.

Photo: Wales Tourist Board.
Sponsored by Snowdon Mountain Railway.

Llyn Peris,
Dinorwig Lower Reservoir.

Photo and sponsored by First Hydro.

Conwy Falls, specially
constructed fish pass nearby.

*Photo and sponsored
by the Environment Agency.*

Snowdon Summit.

Photo: Ieuan Owen.
Sponsored by Great Lakes Chemical Ltd.

Manon Evans and brother Gethin, Holland Arms Garden Centre, Christmas 1995.
Photo: Derec Owen. Sponsored by Garden Centre.

Caernarfon Castle Square, *c.* 1900.

University of Wales, Bangor. Students relaxing by the Memorial Arch. The inscription on this building, in memory of the heroes of the Great War, was designed by Sir John Morris-Jones.
Photo: John Wyn Jones. Sponsored by the University of Wales, Bangor.

Menai Suspension Bridge. *Photo: Ieuan Owen.*
Sponsored by Eastman Chemical Limited Peboc.

Over Menai a structure of strength
On a fine design the seal,
Above the wild waters a form,
A poem in stone and steel.

At night a lifeline lit up,
Golden arches, ambers on high,
Reflections dance on the sea
That mirrors a violet sky.

The Square, Porthaethwy (Menai Bridge), *c.* 1900. Trinity House with white awning.
Sponsored by Midland Bank, Menai Bridge.

Construction of the Tubular Bridge over the Menai Straits (1849). *Courtesy of Ironbridge Gorge Museums. Sponsored by Railtrack.*

HMS Conway in the Mersey with Mauritania, Kenneth Shoesmith, *c.* 1935. Originally HMS Nile, she was built in 1827, a two decker with 92 guns (240 feet long). Renamed Conway in 1876.

Photograph reproduced with the kind permission of the Trustees of the Ulster Museum and the Furness Withy Group. Sponsored by Menter Môn.

This steam engine, originally meant for pulling a plough, was acquired in 1918 by the Llanfair Pwllgwyngyll Co-operative Society. It was then used with a threshing machine in the vicinity and later by Jack Hughes, Bob Carmel's father in the Llannerch-y-medd area and became the property of Captain Hewitt who was known as the Modest Millionaire and lived near Cemlyn. From 1968 until 1991 it was owned and restored by Mr Anthony Phillips, Rhoscolyn and it is still brought to the Anglesey Steam Rally. It is the engine featured in the famous Welsh children's book *Llyfr Mawr y Plant 1* by Jennie Thomas and J.O. Williams to illustrate 'Amser Dyrnu' (Threshing Time). Illustration by Peter Fraser.

Sponsored by the Anglesey Vintage Equipment Society.

Gentle Giants; mare and foal at the Anglesey Show. *Photo: Anglesey Agricultural Society. Sponsored by Farmers Union of Wales.*

Benllech Beach. *Photo: G E Lees (co-operation Robert Williams, Magma).*

Porthmadog Harbour. *Photo: Gwynedd County Council.*

Harlech Castle and sprinter train. *Photo: Ieuan Owen.*

Barmouth viaduct. *Photo: Ieuan Owen.*

Dolgellau. *Photo: Gwynedd County Council.*

Stwlan reservoir, Tanygrisiau. *Photo: Gwynedd County Council.*

During the second half of the 20th century North West Wales has been influential in pushing this process forward. Liberal members namely Megan Lloyd George (Anglesey) and Emrys Roberts (Meirionnydd) were strongly in favour of devolution and it has been a central part of the Liberal Democrat policy for years. Labour leaders after 1945 who campaigned for a Parliament for Wales and who became MPs include Cledwyn Hughes (Anglesey), Goronwy Roberts (Caernarfon), T W Jones (Meirionnydd), Elwyn Jones and Ednyfed Hudson Davies (Conwy). Huw Morris Jones and Gwilym Prys Davies were supporters as well as Wil Edwards and Elystan Morgan who represented Meirionnydd and Ceredigion respectively. Cledwyn Hughes held Anglesey from 1951 to 1979 and became Secretary of State for Wales (1966-68). The recently elected member for Conwy, Betty Williams, is in the same tradition.

Three of the four parliamentary seats have been gained by Plaid Cymru; Dafydd Wigley (Caernarfon) from 1974, Dafydd Elis Thomas (Meirionnydd Nant Conwy) from 1974 until 1992 followed by Elfyn Llwyd, and Ieuan Wyn Jones (Ynys Môn) from 1987.

Sir Wyn Roberts and the Conservatives were opposed to devolution but, after the referendum, they now accept the situation and are campaigning for representation in the Assembly. These are all Welsh speakers and strong supporters of the language while Keith Best the Englishman who was the Conservative member for Anglesey from 1979 to 1987 learned Welsh successfully.

In September 1997, one hundred and two years after the Liberal 'Home Rule all round' stance, the people of Wales, in a referendum, with the wholehearted and honourable support of the Labour leaders, decided in favour of limited devolution not including legislative or tax-varying powers as was decided for Scotland earlier in the same year.

URDD GOBAITH CYMRU - BALA

Another aspect of the national reawakening was the founding in 1922 by Ifan ab Owen Edwards, the son of the above named O M Edwards, of **Urdd Gobaith Cymru** (The Welsh League of Youth) to promote the Welsh language and identity. One of their camps on the shore of Llyn Tegid (Bala Lake), the largest natural lake in Wales, between **Bala** and **Llanuwchllyn** has been a holiday centre for many thousands of young people, both fluent speakers and learners over many years. The largest reservoir in Wales is also near Bala, i.e. Llyn Celyn.

Bala has three monuments, a bronze of Lewis Edwards, Principal of Bala Calvinist Methodist College for 50 years, by Goscombe John; a marble statue of Thomas

Charles one of the eminent leaders of the Calvinistic Methodists and one of the founders of the British and Foreign Bible Society by William Davies outside Tegid chapel; and a bronze full-length statue of Thomas Edward Ellis by Goscombe John in the High Street. There is also a plaque to Mari Jones (1784-1866) the sixteen year old girl who walked from Llanfihangel-y-Pennant near Abergynolwyn to Bala, a forty mile journey to buy a bible from the Rev Thomas Charles. He did not have a spare copy and seeing her great disappointment he gave her his own. At Capel y Pandy, Llanuwchllyn at the entrance to the cemetery, there is a gate of fine iron work by R L Gapper in memory of Sir O M Edwards depicting the angel of the resurrection having conquered death. There is also a monument to both together, the father and son.

REMEMBER TRYWERYN

It is one of the great ironies of the 20th century that in this area, Penllyn, a few miles from Bala, the cradle of modern Welsh nationalism, Liverpool Corporation was able to drown the Tryweryn valley, getting a bill through parliament in the face of almost unanimous opposition by the Welsh members. The big question was: what kind of democracy is it that supports a powerful city against the united will of a nation?

LLANFAIR PWLLGWYNGYLL SCHOOLS

To return to Sir John Morris-Jones's home village the history of the elementary schools in the area is again typical of what was happening elsewhere in Wales. Before 1871 there was a National school at Llanedwen on the outskirts of the village, the Duchess of Kent School, where John Morris-Jones spent the first years of his education. The attractive old building on the Brynsiencyn road, built of buff coloured stone has been converted into two houses called Victoria Cottages. Around 1870 there was bitter controversy between the Liberal Nonconformists and the Tory Church of England supporters over elementary education. The result was that in 1871 a Board School was established and built where the snooker room now stands. The animosity continued and in 1872 another new school, the National (Church) School was built. David Lloyd George later led in the continuing conflict between the supporters of the Church of England and State schools.

THE MEMORIAL HALL

In 1911 a new Council School was built and the old Board School building remained unoccupied. After 1918 it was extended to form the Memorial Hall. Inside there is a low relief stone sculpture of the head of Sir John Morris-Jones by R L Gapper who was also responsible for the gravestone in Llanfair churchyard. The reason why there is another memorial after the Great War in the form of a village clock is that a feud developed between the organizers.

THE SILENT LIONS

Two of the famous four ornamental stone lions at the entrances to the old Tubular Bridge are in Llanfair. But not so well known are the four sphinx-like figures on a railway bridge on the Plas Llanfair drive with two more nearer the main building. It seems probable that Lord Clarence Paget who made the Nelson monument from concrete was responsible for these figures as well.

LONG LIVE THE KING

On the letter box opposite the toll house, instead of the usual letters ER, (Elizabeth Regina) the old GR have been left. George V died in 1936 and George VI, the father of Her Majesty the Queen in 1952.

THE BLUE STONE

On the main road through Llanfair and along the A5 there are semicircular recesses in the wall, where before the age of tarmacadam, the stone breaker used to sit working diligently breaking stones to cobble size for the road surface. In Llanfair one can be seen by Pen Lôn Llan not far from the old small quarry at Bryn Cyrff. A deserted quarry and a poor stone breaker, they sound so insignificant. But according to Edward Greenly, the authority on the geology of Anglesey, whose grave is near the entrance to Llangristiolus church, the blue-grey very hard rock here is quite extraordinary. The 'glaucophane schist' is unique because it has not been found anywhere else in Great Britain. In the Aethwy area it extends from the column for about two square miles towards Dyfnïa, Felin Engan and Castellior.

RELIGIOUS REVIVAL

In the same year as the tragedy of the *Royal Charter*, 1859, there was a very powerful religious revival in Wales. It started in Cardiganshire under the influence of a Wesleyan minister, Mr Humphrey Jones, who had started preaching in America. His preaching deeply affected a Calvinistic minister in the same area, the Rev Dafydd Morgan who was instrumental in spreading the enthusiasm throughout Wales. After the dramatic initial excitement the revival had a lasting effect on many and there was a remarkable increase in chapel membership. The great eloquent preachers attracting large congregations. were popular heroes; the Revs John Elias and Christmas Evans before the 1859 revival and around the turn of the century the Revs John Williams, Brynsiencyn and Thomas Charles Williams of Menai Bridge to name but a few. The preachers were the most powerful and influential leaders of the 19th century and it was from that background that David Lloyd George emerged.

In the same year, 1859, Charles Darwin published *The Origin of Species* causing a great controversy amongst Christians.

LLANFAIR PWLLGWYNGYLL UPPER VILLAGE - GORS WEN

As Llanfair developed around the station, the old village came to be known as Pentre Uchaf (Upper Village). It consisted of a few terraced houses and smallholdings around a marsh called Gors Wen (White Marsh). One of the fields of the former smallholding Tyddyn Ddeici was called Llain Gorswen (Gorswen paddock) and in a book about the history of Wesleyan Methodism in Wales, based on the recollections of a minister, the Rev John Williams, Siglen, Llanfair Pwllgwyngyll, it is recorded that in 1805, two brothers-in-law, Richard Roberts and Captain M'kensie built a chapel in Gors Wen at their own expense. The name remains on one of the houses.

In addition, the book gives some information about the chapels in Llanfair. In 1839 there was some disagreement among members of the Calvinistic chapel nearby and some left to form an Independent church. The Wesleyans sold their chapel to the Independents, this being now the meeting place of the Congregationalists, and built a new one on the new main road. There was a Wesleyan chapel, Salem, until the 1970's, by the site of the Kwik Save shop. There were two chapels very close to each other in the upper village in the early part of the 19th century. The first Calvinistic chapel was built in 1785 where Bryn Golau houses are now situated and before that time services were held in the farmhouse, Dryll y Bowl, nearby. The present large Presbyterian chapel, Rhos y Gad, was built in 1873. There used to be a pew reserved for children from the Home for orphans in Llanfair and when Lloyd George came to the wedding of John Morris-Jones's daughter, the pioneer of the welfare state inadvertently went to sit in this particular pew.

There was one famous Welsh Wesleyan minister who was born and brought up in Llanfair, David Williams, Siglen (1785-1862). He was an outstanding preacher and was known as Dafydd Frenin (King David). He was buried in Smithdown Road cemetery, Liverpool. His brother John, mentioned above, also a minister, wrote about the history of Welsh Wesleyan Methodism.

Summer house at Graig, first home of Women's Institute.
Woodcut Mrs Jagger

PENMYNYDD NEAR LLANFAIR PWLLGWYNGYLL

ENGLISH ROYAL CONNECTIONS

It was in connection with Llywelyn the Great and Llywelyn the Last Prince that the **Tudur (Tudor) family of Penmynydd** first came into prominence. **Ednyfed Fychan**, from Rhos, the area around Colwyn Bay, the steward, who was the foremost officer, right hand man, counsellor and administrator, was generously rewarded and became the founder of a wealthy, land-owning family. Two of his sons, Goronwy and Tudur, were equally loyal and efficient in their service although other younger members of the family were on the side of the English king in 1282. Gruffydd, Ednyfed's third son and his two sons Rhys and Hywel were on Edward I's side in 1277, while the son of Rhys, Sir Gruffydd Llwyd was a loyal servant in the court of Edward II. At the beginning of the 14th century Ednyfed's family were firm supporters of Edward II.

The period of Welsh independence came to an end with the death of Llywelyn y Llyw Olaf (Last Prince) in 1282 and the subsequent conquest by Edward I which involved building the famous castles at Caernarfon, Conwy, Harlech and lastly Beaumaris. After 1284 the western part of Wales became the personal property of the King of England and was called the Principality. It was much later in 1536 that Wales was incorporated into the English state under Henry VIII.

Even after the conquest there was unrest because the Welsh were treated unfairly and Madog ap Llywelyn led a revolt in 1294. Caernarfon castle was taken and there were victories all over Wales. The church and probably the town as well at Llanfaes were burned. This was the beginning of the end for Llanfaes which had been the most important urban settlement in Gwynedd.

Throughout the 13th and 14th centuries, during the reigns of Edward I and II, the Anglesey descendants of Ednyfed Fychan were able to maintain their position as important landowners and influential officials under the crown. They can be regarded as civil servants whose family tradition was to serve the ruler in power. But they were not mere time-servers. They were courageous men showing qualities of leadership. The member of the family who gave them the name 'Tudor' was noted for his boldness. His name was Tudur ap Goronwy but he decided to call himself 'Sir Tudur'. This is how David Fraser relates the consequences: 'When summoned before Edward III to explain why he dared assume knighthood without authority, he replied that he possessed the three necessary qualifications according to the laws of King Arthur. "I am a gentleman" he said, "I have enough estate, and thirdly I am valiant and adventurous!" Then he added, "If my valour and hardiness be doubted of, lo, here I throw down my glove and for due proof of my courage,

I am ready to fight with any man, whatever he be". At which the king, admiring his spirit , made him a knight on the spot'. It is too simplistic to condemn as traitors these Welshmen who supported the English conqueror because politics has always been a combination of self interest and loyalty to a cause. Desire for the acquisition of land and positions of power has generally been the driving force behind the actions of the nobility.

After Sir Tudur's death in 1367 his sons owned estates in Anglesey; Goronwy at Penmynydd, Ednyfed at Trecastell near Llangoed, Rhys at Erddreiniog near Llangefni and Gwilym at Clorach near Llannerch-y-medd. Of these Goronwy was the most prominent. He fought for Edward III and his son Edward the Black Prince in France during the Hundred Years' War (1338-1453) and made his name as a soldier. He and his brother Ednyfed died by drowning in Kent in 1382.

GORONWY AP TUDUR

Goronwy's corpse was brought home and buried at the Franciscan friary in Llanfaes. Later, during the dissolution of the monasteries under Henry VIII, the altar tomb of Goronwy and his wife Myfanwy was moved to the parish church in Penmynydd. The tomb with recumbent effigies of the two, all in alabaster, is elaborate and indicates their high social position. The effigy of Goronwy is of a knight in 14th century armour and that of Myfanwy, a lady in the costume of the period. Both have their hands in prayer and their heads resting on cushions held by two angels. Their daughter, Morfudd, married Gwilym ap Gruffydd, a distant relative, of Penrhyn near Bangor. They owned extensive lands of the Penmynydd family including Llwyn y Moel later Plas Newydd.

MAREDUDD AP TUDUR

Less is known about another brother Maredudd ap Tudur. In 1391 he was a local official and he held land in Anglesey. He is interesting because he was the father of Owain Maredudd who decided to adopt the name of his grandfather and thus became Owain Tudur who married King Henry V's young widow, Catherine of Valois. As the poets of the time refer to Owain as Owain of Anglesey and Penmynydd it is possible that his father lived there after Goronwy's wife and son died towards the end of the 14th century and it is reasonable to assume that Owain was born at Plas Penmynydd. However there is a record that Maredudd's lands and those of his wife were forfeited in 1407 and given to an Englishman as punishment for his support of Owain Glyndŵr. Like the brave and adventurous brothers Goronwy and Ednyfed, the three remaining brothers, Rhys, Gwilym and Maredudd were supporters of Richard II, (1377-1399) and held important offices under the crown. Members of the family were landowners in many parts of North

Wales and one of them, a distant member, Gwilym ap Gruffydd, mentioned above, later associated with the Penrhyn estate near Bangor, held important offices under the crown and became a powerful landowner when the Penmynydd family fell on hard times after supporting Owain Glyndŵr.

Welsh noblemen who were brave professional soldiers and their troops played a prominent part in the Hundred Years' War against France (1338-1453) for Edward III and his son Prince Edward the Black Prince, who died in 1376. With spears and long bows they were crucial at the battles of Crecy, Poitiers and Agincourt.

NATIONAL UPRISING UNDER OWAIN GLYNDŴR

The allegiance of the Penmynydd men came to an end with the uprising of Glyndŵr in the first decade of the 15th century. They were first cousins of Owain and they supported him throughout his campaign which was a great national uprising. When that ultimately failed, they, with many other Welsh people were punished and had their lands forfeited. Penmynydd and Trecastell have been described as 'the island nursery of Welsh nationalism during this period'. On the other hand Gwilym ap Gruffydd, their kinsman, changed sides when he realized that Glyndŵr's campaign was on the decline. In return for his support for the English king he was able to keep his own lands and gain possession of most of the Tudor properties. Penmynydd was his favourite home. At the same time many Welshmen felt that they were second class citizens in their own country because of legal restrictions and because powerful English landowners held important official positions while the English burgesses wanted to cling to their privileges. Some members of leading Welsh families, among them Gwilym Fychan of Penrhyn, the son of Gwilym ap Gruffydd, in 1439, went as far as to seek and obtain the status of an English person. As always, personal gain was in clear focus while any concept of nationhood in the modern sense was vague and confused.

OWAIN TUDUR

The revolt under Glyndŵr had started in 1400. Owain Tudur was born around the same time. It has been suggested that he was present as a young soldier at Agincourt in 1415. Gwilym ap Gruffydd of Penrhyn, the member of the Penmynydd family who had secured royal patronage and had become a powerful landowner at the expense of his kinsmen after the Glyndŵr revolt, died in 1431. Up until that time his favourite home was Penmynydd. One wonders whether in the tortuous history of this family there was a connection between his influence and Owain Tudur's access to the Royal Court. After the death of Henry V in 1422 he was a courtier at Windsor where the handsome young fellow was known as the Rose of Anglesey. He was appointed to the household of the infant Henry VI.

OWAIN MARRIES CATHERINE

Catherine of Valois, the daughter of the king of France was only twenty years old when her husband, King Henry V, died. The handsome courtier Owain had caught the young widow's eye. There is a story that he first came to her notice through his attempt to seduce one of her ladies-in-waiting. The Queen, having found out the proposed rendezvous went there in disguise with the intention of teaching him a lesson. But he was the grandson of Sir Tudur ap Goronwy and instead of reprimanding him she fell in love with him. They were secretly married in 1429 and had four children including Edmund and Jasper Tudor. In the court of Henry VI in 1453 Edmund was made Earl of Richmond and Jasper Earl of Pembroke. In 1455 Edmund married Margaret Beaufort of the house of Lancaster and the red rose. She was the great grand-daughter of John of Gaunt.

Owain Tudur, after some tribulations, received royal support and patronage. As a man in his sixties in 1461 he took part on the side of Lancaster in the Battle of Mortimer's Cross near Leominster. Following a victory for the white rose of York, Owain was captured and taken to Hereford where he was executed. They ripped off the collar of his red velvet doublet ready for the axe. His last words were: 'That head shall be in the stock that was wont to lie on Queen Catherine's lap'. Commending his soul to almighty God he died with dignity.

FATHER DIES BEFORE BIRTH OF SON

Owain Tudur's son, Edmund, Earl of Richmond had died in 1456 before his father. A baby boy was born to Margaret his wife at Pembroke in January 1457. The little boy, Henry, never saw his father but he had a great friend in his uncle, Jasper who devoted his life to his care and career.

THE MEN OF HARLECH

Jasper Tudor depended largely on Wales for support but was always on the move, stirring up trouble and seeking help in Brittany, Ireland and Scotland. His stronghold was Harlech castle. For seven years 1461-1468 fifty of his brave supporters resisted the Yorkist enemy there. It was to his tough garrison that the famous war song 'The march of the men of Harlech' was dedicated.

At a formative period in his life until he was fourteen Henry grew up in different parts of Wales and probably knew Welsh. Then he and Jasper fled to Brittany where they spent many years. After many setbacks and valuable experience, dearly bought, there appeared a window of opportunity in 1485. Henry was twenty eight years old. They had friends in Wales, some help from the king of France, Breton soldiers and men who had fled from the cruelty (according to Tudor propagandists) of the unpopular King Richard III, to form the nucleus of an army. They set sail from the mouth of the Seine bound for Milford Haven on the first of August 1485.

TO BOSWORTH FIELD

Henry Tudor, Earl of Richmond, representing the aspirations of Wales as well as the house of Lancaster, and Jasper his uncle were on Welsh soil and ready for the long march to Bosworth to meet Richard, the 'Black Boar'.

On their way through Wales towards Shrewsbury they were joined by their allies. They proceeded towards Stafford, Lichfield and Tamworth at a fast pace to the field of battle south of Market Bosworth in Leicestershire in the heart of England. There were men from all parts of Wales, including Henry's kinsmen from Gwynedd, marching under the banner of Wales, the red dragon on a white and green background, some on horseback, some on foot. Richard was in the thick of the battle. He was defeated and killed on the field as were many of his foremost supporters.

HENRY CROWNED KING OF ENGLAND

The crown of England was picked up from beneath a hawthorn bush and placed on the head of the grandson of Owain Tudur of Penmynydd, Môn. He was crowned King Henry VII on the battle field. On his knees he thanked God for the victory and prayed that he would rule justly. He behaved like a king and knighted eleven supporters without delay.

During his reign Henry did not draw attention to himself and he was not an innovator. He worked patiently to restore order and good government. Instead of the waste of war he brought prosperity for himself and to the kingdom. It has been claimed that he was possibly the cleverest man who sat on the English throne. But he was not popular having the reputation of being a miserly man. In 1486 Henry married Elizabeth the daughter of Edward IV of York, thus laying down solid foundations for the Tudor dynasty which was to last 118 years. The Tudors included Henry VII, Henry VIII, Edward VI, Mary and Elizabeth I. During the Wars of the Roses some of the nobles had become too powerful thus weakening the King of England's position. But one result of the wars was that many of the barons had been killed and others had become impoverished as a result of their campaigns. Henry VII, with the support of the church, was able to extend his authority.

A whispered word will weigh with the wise - Welsh proverb

NEW WORLD

His reign coincided with the influence of the Renaissance in Britain, particularly through the great scholar Erasmus. They were exciting times too because of the voyages of discovery. Christopher Columbus had discovered the West Indies for Spain in 1492. In 1497 Henry encouraged John Cabot and his son to sail from Bristol in an attempt to reach the Far East and they discovered Newfoundland or Nova Scotia. Henry to some extent founded the Royal Navy. He had two large ships built for it, the *Regent* and the *Sovereign* each of 700 tons displacement, the *Regent* having 225 guns. Also he was responsible for building the first dry dock at Portsmouth.

WESTMINSTER ABBEY

The most remarkable monument to Henry VII is the chapel called after him in Westminster Abbey. It is in fact the Lady chapel and replaced an earlier one dedicated to the Blessed Virgin Mary in 1220. In the perpendicular style, this chapel which is the size of a church has a magnificent fan-vaulted ceiling and contains the ornate tomb of King Henry VII and Queen Elizabeth. The chapel has been claimed one of the most beautiful buildings in the world. Elizabeth of York died in 1503 and Henry in 1509 at the age of fifty two. Their tomb contains effigies of the king and queen, the work of the Florentine sculptor Pietro Torrigiano. There is a small oil painting of Henry VII by an unknown Netherlands artist painted in 1505 at the National Portrait Gallery in London. There is also a fine statue, one of eleven called the Heroes of Wales, in the City Hall, Cardiff, installed in 1916. Amongst others included are St David, Llywelyn the Last Prince, and Owain Glyndŵr.

HENRY - A WELSHMAN?

Although Henry had been brought up in Wales and probably knew Welsh, and despite the fact that he was proud of the Welsh Dragon and called his son Arthur he did not have a clear perception of Wales as a nation. He spent most of his adult life in Brittany and France. He had a claim to the throne of England and that was the greater prize for himself and the supporters of the Lancastrian cause.

But over the years the continual attacks by the English and the Normans had forced some of our own soldier-kings and nobles to think in terms of Welsh nationality and co-operation. This was reinforced by the harsh treatment of the Welsh people in reprisals after insurrections.

Even after the conquest of 1282 there was much unrest and in 1294, as was mentioned earlier, there was a concerted rebellion under Madog of Gwynedd.

Facing the reality of their sad plight and angered by years of arrogant, bad foreign government Wales was united in revolt. The Welsh soldiers fought hard and took many castles throughout the country including the fortress at Caernarfon but were defeated in the end by Edward's superior forces. It was the best planned campaign until the uprising under Owain Glyndŵr at the end of another century and undoubtedly served as an inspiration to William Wallace who led the Scottish revolt two years later. Before the battle of Stirling Bridge in 1298 he sent the English ambassadors home with the words: 'We Scots did not come here to negotiate but to fight and set Scotland free'. After this serious revolt under Madog of the Gwynedd royal line Edward started building Beaumaris Castle. He then established the borough and brought in a large number of English people. The charter granted to the borough in 1296 meant that the English settlers were given all kinds of rights and privileges at the expense of the Welsh of the old town of Llanfaes nearby. In 1303 the Welsh people were forced out of their town and settled in Rhosyr thereafter called Newborough.

ANGLICIZATION UNDER THE TUDORS

Welsh identity had become clearer during the uprising of Owain Glyndŵr a century after the conquest. At least the leader, Glyndŵr had a vision of Wales with its own independent church with Welsh-speaking bishops and priests, its own parliament and two universities. But unfortunately Henry VII, although his ancestors of Penmynydd had fought on the side of Glyndŵr, having won the great prize of the throne of England, was unable to appreciate the real situation of Wales and the sad plight of its people. Perhaps it would be fairer to deduce that if he did so, events did not allow him to do more than he did. He rewarded generously the friends and collaborators who had fought for him and he lifted the many restrictions on Welshmen with regard to property, rights, and the holding of offices. And he re-established the Council of Wales and the Marches meeting at a convenient central position in Ludlow. He secured a much greater measure of law and order and provided greater opportunities for the Welsh landowning gentry. Henry VIII, mainly through the Acts of Union of England and Wales, 1536-42 accelerated this process. It was enacted that English would be the official language of the courts and that knowledge of English was essential for any post under the crown. Since most of the people spoke only Welsh, there must have been translators in the courts but the net result from both clauses was that the Welsh were second class citizens in their own country.

UNION WITH ENGLAND

The social and political results of these Acts have been condemned as catastrophic by many patriotic writers and one can at least claim that another option was available to the Welsh king of England, that is, to build on the ideas laid down by Owain Glyndŵr giving the Principality self-government and dominion status so that it could develop into a responsible nation and the nearest ally to England. It is easy to suggest such alternatives with the benefit of hindsight but the king and his advisers operated under the complicated circumstances and centralising theories of their time. Curiously, the acts did give Wales some administrative distinction and defined her boundaries more clearly than before.

Hugh Thomas in *A History of Wales 1485-1660* draws attention to the ambitious Welsh families. 'They had taken advantage of English laws to further their own ends. They had dispatched their sons to the courts of the king or the marcher lords to be educated. This inevitably implied the assimilation of English attitudes and a mastery of the English language. A few enrolled their sons at English schools, at the English universities of Oxford and Cambridge, and at the Inns of Court, where they completed their education with the study of English law. All this could not fail to leave its mark upon the attitudes of the most capable and ambitious among the Welsh'. In his introduction he had written: 'But all this was bought at a price. ... Between the few who had and the many who had not, sympathy and understanding declined as the gap became wider'. It should be remembered that for the two Henrys one priority was to give the English language official status in situations where Latin had reigned supreme and that under Queen Elizabeth in 1563 Parliament passed a law that there should be a Bible translated into Welsh available in every church in Wales by St David's Day 1567, albeit beside the English version.

The nobility, the natural and traditional leaders of the people gradually turned towards London and became Anglicized with the result that their families became strangers in their own country.

Queen Victoria on a visit to Llanfair Bridge.

SCENERY AND GEOLOGY

SCENERY

The most significant visible features of this area of North Wales are the mountain peaks of Snowdonia together with the valleys and lakes formed by glaciers during the Ice Age which lasted until about 10,000 years ago and covered most of Northern Europe. A number of people, mainly visitors, have climbed to the summit of Snowdon in the evening or at night in order to have the memorable experience of seeing the sun rising in a rose-tinted sky on the horizon over distant hilltops. But on a fine evening, whatever the season, and particularly during frosty weather, thousands of people, young and old, look to the west over Llŷn and Anglesey and gaze in wonder at the great drama of the sunset with a wide pink sky and bars of orange and gold above a headland or the darkening sea. There are magnificent views from the hills above Harlech, over the Straits and Anglesey from Y Felinheli and many other places while one very special look out point is the lay-by on the heather-covered heath near Rhosgadfan. On the wall of this parking and picnic spot designed by the sculptor Jonah Jones are inscribed in Welsh and English these words: 'This view has refreshed the spirit of many and inspired the writings of Kate Roberts of Rhosgadfan 1891-1985'.

RECENT MARKS ON THE LANDSCAPE

QUARRIES

The scenery gives great joy but many of us tend to take more notice of the large-scale marks left on the landscape through human activities. Of these the most spectacular are the slate quarries. We can see the series of terraces and huge galleries of the Penrhyn (Bethesda) and Dinorwig (Llanberis) quarries the first of which is still working and the deep wide pits in the Nantlle valley. There are several beds of these Cambrian Age slates, first formed about six hundred million years ago but metamorphosed or changed by heat and pressure about two hundred million years later, running in a North East to South West direction from Bethesda to Dyffryn Nantlle. They are blue, grey or reddish-purple in colour with a few green veins and patches of green showing on individual roofing slates. About 10.5 miles (17km) south-west of Betws-y-coed lies the important slate area of Blaenau Ffestiniog where some of the open quarries are still producing while some of the mines with their large caverns have been converted into tourist attractions. In all the areas there are mountainous waste tips showing the extent of the excavation. It has been claimed that the Penrhyn and Dinorwig quarries were the largest in the world and that the best slates in the world have been obtained from North Wales.

The industry started with small groups of smallholders, following a tradition of working on outcrops for personal or local need, during the 18th century, making small quarries at Cilgwyn in Dyffryn Nantlle, on the eastern slopes of Llyn Padarn, Llanberis and on the hillsides around Llanllechid and Bethesda. The methods were primitive and for transport they used pack-horses and mules and sledges. Early in the 18th century there was increasing trade to growing towns and cities so that in 1721 more than two million slates were exported to Chester, Liverpool, South Wales and abroad from Caernarfon. During the first part of the 19th century large landowners took over and developed the industry on a massive scale, with the result that sparsely populated uplands suddenly developed into very large villages or towns as happened in Dyffryn Ogwen. There a few people built a small Independent chapel and called it Bethesda and within a few decades, with a swollen population of about 6,000 the chapel was rebuilt twice. This was replicated in other quarrying areas hence the fascinating phenomenon of having villages with the biblical names, Carmel, Saron, Seion and Bethel in Caernarfonshire although they are not restricted to this area. During the second half of the 19th century production reached its peak, school writing slates and other products as well as roofing slates being exported not only from Caernarfon which originally had a virtual monopoly but from the new harbours, Porth Penrhyn, Y Felinheli becoming Port Dinorwig and Porthmadog. Meanwhile the men were working under very hard conditions, agitation grew and, mainly through the leadership of W J Parry of Bethesda, a union for all the principal quarries of North Wales was formed. The century came to a very sad end through the intimidating action of the intransigent quarry owner, the man who was the second Lord Penrhyn after 1886, who died in 1907. In 1900 he let parts of the quarry to outside contractors thereby infuriating the workers. Because some of them tried to force the contractor's men from the quarry twenty six men had to appear in court in Bangor charged with assault. They were stoutly defended by David Lloyd George and his brother William George. Twenty one of the men were acquitted and the others fined only. The great strike or lock-out of 1900 lasted three years making it the longest industrial dispute, and despite the solidarity of most of the workers, in the end they were beaten by hunger and hopelessness, the bitterness still remaining.

Production was at its peak in the 19th century when 3,000 to 4,000 men and boys were employed in the industry. After a very marked decline there is again considerable production by modern methods. This is how Professor E G Bowen, described the social impact: 'The overwhelming strength of Nonconformity was clearly associated with the industry, and the chapels in turn were instrumental in bringing about a very close integration of the religious, educational, artistic and political aspects of life. It was the chapels, with the schools, reading rooms, libraries and eisteddfodau, that knit together a people who lacked an urban tradition. These institutions served also as valuable training grounds for future leaders in all branches of public life'. He went on to emphasize the importance of the quarrymen's huts near their place of work where they had their mid-day meal, the 'caban' where brief but sometimes high quality discussions about matters of the day were held, some of the men being very able and articulate. An outstanding example was the Rev John Jones, Talysarn (1796-1857). He was born in Dolwyddelan, worked on the Capel Curig, Llyn Ogwen road and later in the Talysarn slate quarry. Self-educated, he became one of the most powerful preachers of his denomination, the Calvinistic Methodists.

The same could be said about the granite quarries of Penmaen-mawr and Yr Eifl as well as the limestone quarries at Penmon, Anglesey and Llanddulas and others near Colwyn Bay.

Penmaen-mawr, one of the largest granite quarries in the British Isles is still very busy producing mainly crushed stone but the same cannot be said about the granite quarries near Trefor in the Llŷn Peninsula which used to produce kerb stones and the small rectangular blocks known as 'setts' for road surfacing. The pink and blue-grey stone has been used for monumental purposes and for curling stones, quarried at Trefor and sent to Degannwy for shaping. Ioan Mai of Llithfaen nearby has drawn attention to the fact that there is a connection between 'Coronation Street' and the Welsh 'Minafon' soap series in that the cobbled street in both have been made with setts from the quarries of Llŷn. Setts used to be produced at Penmaen-mawr as well.

The one place in Anglesey which shows the result of industrial exploitation in a dramatic way is Mynydd Parys where there has been extensive excavation for copper. It consists of a great opencast pit together with deep mines and waste tips. Another feature are the shallow precipitation pits in which water containing metal sulphates was collected in order to dump scrap iron into them to give the ferric oxide that has given the rust colour to the whole area. Incidentally, the same chemical has given the characteristic colour to the red sandstone exposed in a few places in Anglesey such as Llugwy, Foel and Moel y Don near to which there is a red sandstone quarry. It seems likely that the well-known mansion Plas Coch, one of the most architecturally pleasing on the island, has been built of this local stone.

FORESTS

There are in Newborough in Anglesey and in Llŷn as well as in many parts of the mainland extensive conifer forests. The Forestry Commission started planting at Coed y Brenin near Dolgellau in 1922 and in 1948 at Newborough. Although these contain magnificent specimens such as, for example, the majestic Douglas Firs in Coed y Brenin, in the past they have been controversial and in recent years more indigenous trees have been grown providing variety and splendid colours in autumn. With road improvements attractive shrubs and trees and thousands of flowers such as daffodils and cowslips have been planted along the verges enhancing the scenery and providing food and cover for wildlife.

LAKES

There are a large number of lakes west of the River Conwy and around Snowdon, as well as the large Llyn Tegid, Llyn Celyn and Llyn Trawsfynydd to the south. Llyn Trawsfynydd is an artificial lake first formed in 1928 for a hydro electricity station near Maentwrog and enlarged during the 1960's when the Nuclear Power Station was built. On Anglesey the lakes are smaller, the one on Mynydd Bodafon with its rocky background and the slopes covered with gorse and heather being very attractive. In *Anglesey and the North Wales Coast* F H Glazebrook wrote: 'It provides perhaps the most perfect piece of inland scenery in the Isle of Anglesey. ... The winding road, the colour-washed cottages conspire to produce a scene of great charm'. The two larger reservoirs Llyn Cefni and Llyn Alaw were made during the middle of the 20th century to provide a water supply for the island.

Some of the lakes have been harnessed to supply electricity. The first was the North Wales Power hydro-electric station at Cwm Dyli using water from Llyn Llydaw, high up under Lliwedd, built in 1905 and still in operation. The Dolgarrog hydro-electric scheme is also from the first part of the 20th century. The Ffestiniog Power Station uses water from the Stwlan reservoir above Tanygrisiau. Completed in 1963 this was the first hydro-electric pumped storage power station to be built in the UK by the old Central Electricity Generating Board. A large 267yd (244m) dam has been built across the end of Llyn Stwlan to provide the high altitude water supply necessary for the water to turn the turbines by gravity. After travelling on foot or by car up the exciting zig zag road on the slopes of Y Moelwyn, the massive dam with its arches is really impressive. The scale of the project, involving the lower reservoir, the power station, the shafts and tunnels may be judged from the fact that it took six years to complete. On a still grander scale is the Dinorwig Pumped Storage Power Station in Llanberis, a scheme utilizing off-peak electricity to pump water from Llyn Peris to the higher reservoir at Marchlyn Mawr, at one of the highest points in Britain, on the other side of the valley from Snowdon. Apart from the essential reservoirs which can be seen, the shafts, tunnels and caverns inside the mountain are on a stupendous scale. The turbines and machinery are in large halls inside Elidir Fawr mountain. The chamber containing the major power machinery is one of the largest caves ever made by man. Its length is twice that of a football pitch and it is half as wide and is 66yd (60m) high. Opened in 1984 this station can supply 1680 megawatts for up to five hours. Within ten seconds it can move from zero to produce 1320 megawatts of power. Water is vital also for the two concrete Magnox nuclear power stations at Wylfa in Anglesey, first commissioned in 1971, and Trawsfynydd, the latter having completed its working life and the other due to be decommissioned within a few years. The National Grid was set up during the nine years after 1926. The power lines from Wylfa, Trawsfynydd, Ffestiniog and Dinorwig run eastwards across North Wales.

Environmental considerations were very important in the Dinorwig project because of its sensitive location. For example, with regard to wildlife Llyn Peris had always been a habitat for salmon, sea trout, brown trout and others including the *Torgoch* (Arctic Char) from the Ice Age. This rare species of the salmon family was found in only four lakes in Wales, Llyn Peris, Llyn Padarn, Bodlyn and Cwellyn. During the construction of the power station it was necessary to widen Llyn Peris and deepen it by removing slate waste that had been deposited in it. This involved draining the lake dry for three years.

To safeguard the *torgoch* some were moved to another suitable lake in Snowdonia, the deep Ffynnon Llugwy Lake and new stock were bred in a hatchery. Special arrangements were made for the salmon and sea trout to be able to go upstream to their usual spawning grounds in Afon Nant Peris.

CASTLES BRIDGES AND WALLS

Comparable in size to the huge concrete buildings of the nuclear power stations are the massive stone-built medieval castles erected by Edward I, prominent on the landscape at Conwy, Caernarfon, Harlech and Beaumaris. And from the 19th century the two famous bridges across the Menai Straits display one aspect of the geology of the area in the massive towers built with huge blocks of limestone from the thick horizontal and cracked beds at Penmon. The breakwater at Holyhead contains local stone and great slabs of limestone from Moelfre. And around the big houses, Penrhyn, Faenol, Plas Newydd and Glynllifon the 10ft (3m) stone walls with the impressive gates and lodges, stand to remind us of a cruel age when there were mantraps and spring guns concealed under the bushes inside against poachers. As Trevelyan says: 'By a new law of 1816, the starving cottager who went out to take a hare or rabbit, for the family pot could be transported for seven years if caught with his nets upon him at night'.

THE GEOLOGY OF THE AREA

Less well-known than the castles, bridges and slate quarries is the great significance of the area from a geological point of view. Wales has been so attractive and instructive for the variety of its rocks that geologists have accepted three important technical terms from our country. Cambrian from Cambria, a Latinate name for Wales, refers to very old, almost the oldest rocks from 600 million years ago, and the term was introduced by the geologist Sir Andrew Crombie Ramsay whose wife, Louisa Mary, was the daughter of the Rev James Williams. James was the son of John Williams, Treffos, Llansadwrn, brother of Thomas Williams (1737-1802), the famous Twm Chwarae Teg who organised the Trysglwyn (Parys) Copper Mine. Ramsay was buried in Llansadwrn. The terms for Ordovician, 500 million, and Silurian, 400 million years ago are derived from the names of Brythonic tribes, the Ordovicians in mid and north Wales and the Silurians in south east Wales and the borders in Roman and pre-Roman times. Anglesey is noted for the oldest rocks of all, the Pre-Cambrian called the Mona Complex. Mynydd Bodafon, it is claimed, is the oldest mountain in Wales, possibly in Europe. No one knows how old these rocks are because there are no clues in the form of fossils in them so it was a time before there was plant or animal life on the land masses and oceans of the primeval earth. They have derived from the intense heat of the earth's crust in a molten state, cooled and solidified but they may have been subjected to tremendous heat and pressure more than once with their character being changed thereby. In Anglesey they make up two thirds of the island's area and are to be seen in West Llŷn, Pembroke, the Highlands and Islands of Scotland, the nearest in England being at Longmynd in Shropshire. There are large areas in Canada, Scandinavia, Siberia, Western Australia and Brazil. As well as these very old hard rocks called 'gneisses' and 'schists' there is a great variety in the island including important limestone deposits and although unexpected and unobtrusive, coal measures at Pentre Berw near Llangefni. The most spectacular geological scenery is at South Stack cliffs near Holyhead where the one time horizontal sedimentary rock beds have been changed by heat and pressure to harder rocks and forced into a wavy pattern like the folds of a fabric by great upheavals of the earth's crust.

FOSSILS

As it is impossible for us to imagine the vastness of space in the universe so it is with the millions of years of geological time. But fossils of all types provide evidence from distant geological ages that make the concept of the world at that time a little more comprehensible. They are pictures or imprints in stone of plants and animals in limestone, coal and slates as we can see in museums. Of these the most dramatic and by today well known examples from their fossils are the dinosaurs or 'terrible lizards' which lived in the warm, humid climate of the swamps and jungles that covered most of the earth. One of the most terrifying was *Tyrannosaurus Rex*, King of the Tyrant Lizards, the forty feet long flesh-eating dinosaur, the terror of the tropical terrain during the Cretaceous Period one hundred and forty four to sixty five million years ago. This monster was the most terrible beast that ever lived on earth. The first complete skeleton of *Tyrannosaurus* was discovered in Montana in 1902. Dinosaurs have been found in the Gobi desert and other places, some in the south of England. It is interesting, because of the Welsh connection,

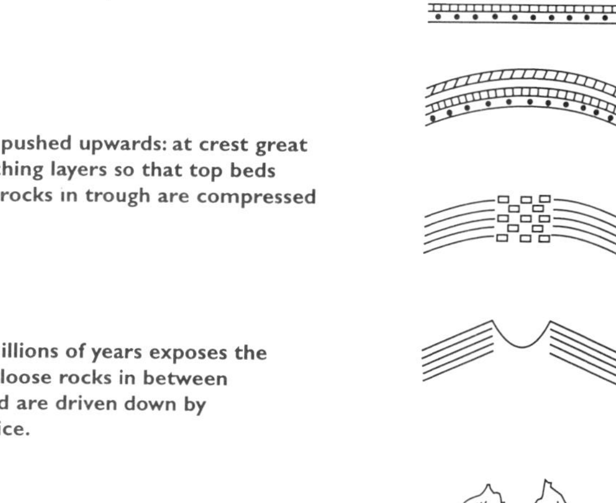

1. Horizontal sedimentary rock beds

2 - 3.
Anticline beds pushed upwards: at crest great pressure stretching layers so that top beds crumble while rocks in trough are compressed and hardened.

4.
Erosion over millions of years exposes the summits while loose rocks in between disintegrate and are driven down by rain, snow and ice.

5.
Near the summits and on slopes there are huge jagged rocks.

Map, Geology of North West Wales *Gwasg Carreg Gwalch* *Diagram formation of mountains* *Stephen Edwards*

that, since 1992, remarkable discoveries have been made in Patagonia, Argentina. *Argentinosaurus huinculensis*, probably the largest plant-eating animal to have lived, weighed over 100 tons while it is claimed that *Giganotosaurus carolinii* was significantly larger than *Tyrannosaurus rex*.

THE ROCKS OF NORTH WEST WALES

Geologists classify rocks into three main types, igneous, sedimentary and metamorphic. Igneous rocks are those that have been formed by heat within the earth's crust; sedimentary rocks have been formed by the pressure of layer upon layer of different materials such as sand and clay on the sea bed; metamorphic rocks are sedimentary or igneous rocks which have been changed or metamorphosed by great heat and pressure. One example of a sedimentary rock is sandstone made from sand deposited on the sea bed while another, coal, now usually deep down in the earth was originally formed from rotting trees and plants, different from the ones we know today, on the surface, then covered with water and layers of solid materials. An example of an igneous rock is granite which was once in a liquid state deep in the earth's hot crust but came up into the surface beds under volcanic conditions, cooled and became a very hard rock. Marble is an example of a metamorphic rock; in its original state it was limestone and became crystalline and harder under pressure and heat. As well as limestone deposited on the sea bed there were layers and layers of shale which by the same process was converted into slate. Had the process continued the slate in its turn could have changed further into a schist, a very hard rock.

CAMBRIAN ROCKS

The Cambrian period started about six hundred million years ago. At this time the pre-Cambrian rocks were probably mountains on the edge of a great sea that covered the area that is now Snowdonia. The process of weathering and erosion of these mountains which resulted in depositing great depths of materials to form Cambrian rocks on the bottom of this ocean continued for a million years. More layers were deposited for another million years in the Ordovician and Silurian periods. During the Ordovician age there was a great deal of volcanic activity when lava and ashes were deposited on the sedimentary rocks of the sea bed. Some of the molten rock trapped in the sedimentary layers became igneous rocks such as granite and dolerite. Later great violent movements of the earth's crust resulted in massive upheaval of the sedimentary beds and igneous rocks.

It is this upheaval that is responsible for the remarkable fact that there are fossils of sea shells on the summit of Snowdon. But it must not be thought that the peaks of Snowdonia and Yr Eifl, though the shapes of some of them are deceptive, were once volcanoes. There was great volcanic activity somewhere in the vicinity but that was under the sea about four hundred and fifty million years ago. How then does one explain the existence of these majestic peaks? As is shown in the diagram on page 119 the parallel and horizontal sedimentary beds under the sea developed into a hump. As this large hump was pushed ever higher the beds at the crest were stretched and in this process the rocks were cracked and crumbled and therefore unstable. In contrast the beds at the trough were subjected to the pressure of compression and were hardened. Over many years the summits suffered continuous erosion and where the bare rock is exposed the strata of the beds are visible at an oblique angle, with the ridges and summits like the jagged edge of a disintegrating basin.

THE ICE AGE

In geological terms the Ice Age was comparatively recent ending about ten thousand years ago. Although not always realized, this geological factor is responsible for very important features of the North Wales landscape. Glaciers from the ice cap, hundreds of feet thick moved downward and outward from the summits bringing down huge rough boulders to the higher slopes, gouging a *cwm*, or amphitheatre, such as Cwm Idwal or Cwm Du'r Arddu out of the mountain sides and pushing along the river valleys which were V-shaped. In so doing the ice carved a U-shaped passage for itself as in Dyffryn Ogwen to Bethesda and down from the top of Llanberis Pass creating the basins for Llyn Peris and Llyn Padarn. At the end of this tremendous sculpturing, ridges and heaps of stones and rubble were left behind damming valleys and basins in places thus creating lakes in some lowlands and others high up in the mountains.

At the same time as the local glaciers were moving down the valleys a very large-scale mass of ice was coming from Scotland and the North where the Irish Sea is now. This covered most of Anglesey and when it met the glaciers from the Arfon mountains there was pressure along the existing valley in a south-westerly and possibly, also, a north-easterly direction carving out a deeper valley which was subsequently flooded and became the Menai Straits. It is said that at the watershed of the original valley between the two bridges there is only ten feet of water.

WHERE PEOPLE LIVE

Parts of Snowdonia remain as they have been from time immemorial, the mountains, their rocky slopes and the lakes, while the landscape in other parts has been fashioned over many centuries by the way of life of the inhabitants. Grazing by sheep, goats, ponies and cattle over a long period, to some extent, has brought the green to the upland pastures. And the people have left their marks, using local materials, in dry stone walls, in small bridges and cottages.

Places have their Welsh names that cling; Llanuwchllyn, Nant Peris, Dyffryn Ardudwy, each like a miniature poem expressing the essence of the place. From the early 6th century, when the Welsh language evolved from the Brythonic and for over a thousand years the only words for the features of the landscape had been Welsh; afon < *abona* (river); dyffryn < *dubrosenton* (valley) or dwfr hynt (water course). Of course there have been borrowings such as pont from the Latin *pontem* (bridge) and cwmwl from *cumulus* (cloud). Throughout this long period Welsh was the language of work and play, of conversation, entertainment and literature, of religion and of life's most sacred moments. When it was spoken every day by all the people it was taken for granted. Today with all the pressure of modern life on it we fully realize that it is in great danger. The people who work to protect the countryside and wildlife do so in the knowledge that it has taken millions of years for this precious heritage to take form. In their intuitive wisdom they work with nature and seek to influence individuals and Government agencies. They should understand how Welsh people feel about the perilous state of the language. In Parc Cenedlaethol Eryri there are living Welsh communities. To sustain the pattern of their lives and livelihood it is necessary to allow carefully controlled building and industrial development with the well-designed infrastructure improvements involved. The human dimension is of primary importance.

EARLY TOURISTS IN SNOWDONIA

The clothes of the early tourists were most unsuitable for venturing up the rocky slopes of Snowdonia. More and more visitors were coming and many of them wanted to climb the highest mountain in England and Wales, Yr Wyddfa, Snowdon at 3,560ft (1,085m) above sea level. The transport facilities available in the form of improved roads, the train, to Bangor in 1848, Caernarfon 1852 and Llanberis 1869, and the steam pleasure boats from Liverpool to Anglesey and Bangor were part of the reason. Men and women from the towns came for the thrill of adventure and to experience the dramatic scenery. Over the years the very names, Crib Goch, Y Lliwedd and Clogwyn Du'r Arddu have fired imaginations, have presented a challenge and many could possibly join Wordsworth saying: 'I have felt a presence that disturbs me with the joy of elevated thoughts'. The early tourists either walked up Snowdon or went on horseback, the horses usually going within half a mile of the summit. It was essential to employ the services of guides, local men who knew the mountains well from boyhood or through their work and who worked in co-operation with the hotels in Llanberis, Beddgelert, and Rhyd Ddu and at Pen-y-pas and Penygwryd. The most famous of the hotels is the Penygwryd on the Capel Curig side of Pen-y-pas, at the top of Llanberis Pass. Starting as a cottage supplying refreshments it developed into a refuge for climbers. Its fame was enhanced when the 1953 Everest expedition led by Sir John Hunt and Dr Charles Evans stayed there while they had a foretaste of the great adventure in the tough winter conditions of Snowdonia. Dr Charles Evans subsequently became the Principal of the University College, Bangor.

SNOWDON AND THE PEAKS

The highest mountain in England and Wales is 3,560ft above sea level. In Snowdonia there are fifteen peaks above 3,000 ft.

Yr Wyddfa	3,560	1,085m
Crib y Ddysgl	3,493	1,065m
Carnedd Llywelyn	3,484	1,064m
Carnedd Ddafydd	3,426	1,044m
Glyder Fawr	3,279	999m
Glyder Fach	3,262	994m
Pen yr Ole Wen	3,210	978m
Foel Grach	3,195	976m
Yr Elen	3,152	962m
Y Garn	3,104	947m
Foel Fras	3,091	942m
Garnedd Uchaf	3,038	926m
Elidir Fawr	3,029	924m
Y Grib Goch	3,026	923m
Tryfan	3,010	915m

There are six public footpaths and other routes to the summit of Snowdon. The usual ones are: the Pig Track or PYG (Penygwryd) starting from the youth hostel or car park; Crib Goch starting from Bwlch y Moch about a mile from Penygwryd; the Miners' Track starting from Pen-y-pas; the Watkin Path from Nant Gwynant; Y Lliwedd Path starting from Pen-y-pas along the miners' track; the Rhyd Ddu Path; the Snowdon Ranger Path (now the youth hostel by Llyn Cwellyn) and the Llanberis Path roughly following the railway track.

One of the most famous routes is what is called 'The Horseshoe'. From the car park at Pen-y-pas the climbers go along the PYG track due west to Grib Goch, along Crib y Ddysgl to Carnedd Igin, then to Bwlch Glas and the summit of Snowdon. The route goes down from the summit and then along the ridge to the top of Lliwedd with Llyn Llydaw on the left below, along the Miners' Track once more and back to Pen-y-pas. It takes about six and a half hours to cover the seven and a half miles (12km).

SAFETY

It is most important that anyone contemplating climbing in Snowdonia should heed the advice given by the wardens and the rescue services. They recommend; strong boots, a rucksack containing essential food and clothing, wind proof and water proof garments, spare sweater, map, compass, whistle, food survival bag. It is not advisable to go alone; one should know the weather forecast before setting out and should leave a note of the route and estimated time of return with a responsible person who could give the necessary information to the rescue services. A survival bag of brightly coloured polythene is a great help to find someone. Signals of distress include six blasts on a whistle, six shouts or six flashes of a torch.

The Llanberis Pass and the less well-known Ceunant Mawr waterfall are two other dramatic features of this valley in contrast with the usually tranquil waters of the two lakes Llyn Padarn and Llyn Peris. The narrow gauge *Llanberis Lake Railway* runs from Gilfach Ddu in Parc Padarn along the whole length of Llyn Padarn to Pen-llyn and back. The *Welsh Slate Museum* in Parc Padarn must not be missed as it provides an insight into the most important industry of North Wales with an opportunity to see a demonstration of slate splitting and dressing by hand. A few yards from the main street one can stroll along the pleasant lakeside paths or on the grass verge or hire a dinghy to row on the lake. One of the Welsh princes' castles, Dolbadarn, stands on the edge of Llyn Peris. As well as this connection with Llywelyn the Great, Llanberis can claim that the ancestors of Thomas Jefferson, third president of the USA and one of the signatories of the Declaration of Independence, came from the area.

SNOWDON ACQUIRED BY NATIONAL TRUST

In August 1998 4,118 acres of land extending to the summit of Snowdon was put up for sale. It is made up of the working hill farm Hafod y Llan together with the neighbouring Gelli Iago. The National Trust campaigned to acquire this important area of countryside for the nation.

The Port Talbot born actor and film star Sir Anthony Hopkins, President of the National Trust Snowdonia Appeal since 1990, in a magnificent gesture, gave a personal donation of £1 million to the Save Snowdon Campaign.

When a job is begun it is two parts done - Welsh proverb

THE CRUEL SEA

TRAETH LAFAN - LLYS HELIG

Between the Beaumaris to Penmon Point part of Anglesey and the mainland there is a vast expanse of sand covered by shallow water for part of the day but exposed at low tide. There is a legend concerning this large sand bank which is similar to other Welsh stories, such as the one about the district of Cantre'r Gwaelod in Cardigan Bay. According to the story there was a big catastrophe when the sea rushed in over the kingdom and palace of Helig ap Glanawg. When the sea came over the land all was lost as retribution for his wrong-doings and the people were drowned. The story possibly encapsulates folk memory from the Stone Age of the geological separation of Anglesey from the mainland. For many years the view was held that certain stones a few miles out to sea in Conwy Bay were the ruins of ancient buildings. Further supporting evidence seemed to be available in stumps and trunks of trees from submerged forests buried in the sand and mud along the coast. As early as the 12th century Giraldus Cambrensis had recorded seeing such trunks with hatchet marks as if only recently felled in St Brides Bay, Pembroke. This was no mystery as they were probably the axe strokes of recent fuel gatherers. The presence of wood preserved in the wet mud is a fact but there is another interpretation of the stone 'walls'. This is the conclusion of F J North in his book *Sunken Cities*: 'Llys helig is not the ruin of human habitation, but an accumulation of stones brought together during the Ice Age and exposed in their present position as a result of erosion and submergence. There has indeed been an encroachment of the sea in the area to which the legend relates'. North concludes that, similarly, the Cantre'r Gwaelod legend is an elaboration of incidents of inundation rather than one great calamity. The Sarnau '... stony banks extending for considerable distances into Cardigan Bay ... which have been indicated as the remains of dams built to keep the sea out of Cantre'r Gwaelod are natural ridges'. The stones at Caer Arianrhod near Dinas Dinlle, Caernarfon are also a natural phenomenon, stones from the boulder clay of the Ice Age. North says further: 'All the available evidence, then, goes to show that there was a time, well within the human era, when the Cardigan Bay we know had not been developed. This confirms the conclusion, arrived at on other grounds, that people living in the region could have been affected by the encroachment of the sea to which the bay owes its origin'. His view is that a combination of wind and waves which affected a few homesteads, grew over centuries to the story of a great catastrophe and he reminds us of the floods around the Severn estuary in 1607 and the widespread flooding of regions of Eastern England in 1953. Residents of the midland counties of England will long remember the catastrophic floods of early 1998.

FLOODS AT TYWYN AND ABERCONWY

On 26 February 1990 North Wales was subjected to the most severe storm in living memory. Sea defences along forty miles of coastline proved completely inadequate against the combined destructive power of storm-force winds and an exceptionally high tide. The promenade at Penmaen-mawr was severely damaged, the sea walls around Llandudno were battered, but the worst hit part was the level low-lying area around Tywyn and Kinmel Bay where a 218yd (200m) stretch of sea wall collapsed resulting in serious flooding over approximately 4 square miles (10sq.km). Caravans were swept along by the wind and the water and many people had to be rescued by boats and helicopters from their homes. There was torrential rain, a howling wind, tempestuous waves, hail, thunder and lightning and the blue flashing lights of emergency service vehicles on the partially flooded roads. The rail track was damaged in places and passengers were transferred to coaches in Chester.

The destruction left by the freak storm at Aberconwy on 10 June 1993 was similar in scale to that at Tywyn earlier. The combination of torrential rain and a high tide created conditions not to be expected within, at least a hundred and sixty years, causing tragic flooding in Morfa Conwy and housing estates in Llandudno and Llandudno Junction. Five inches (12.7cm) of rain fell in three hours, streams and rivers overflowed their banks causing 10ft (3m) floods in Llandudno Junction. Two thousand five hundred people were forced to leave their homes, the Aberconwy Centre serving as an emergency reception centre for victims.

SHIPWRECKS, LIGHTHOUSES AND LIFEBOATS

The Skerries islands off Holyhead and the rocky coasts of Anglesey and Gwynedd have been notoriously dangerous for shipping making it necessary to have the assistance of pilots, locally as in the Straits, and also for large ships and ocean-going liners entering and leaving Liverpool. Near Point Lynas, at the northern tip of Anglesey, pilots for Liverpool ships would be picked up from their pilot boat, a small ship, moored there or coasting in the vicinity. More recently the pilots had a shore station and would use a fast launch but sophisticated navigation equipment has made this type of service largely redundant. Currently there are two launches at Amlwch Port and remote control equipment at Point Lynas enabling staff at Liverpool to receive information about conditions out in Liverpool Bay. When necessary a pilot is driven by taxi from the Wirral to Amlwch Port from where he can go out to a ship wishing to enter the Mersey. There is also a self-employed pilot at Holyhead to provide assistance as necessary for ships coming into the port.

Because of the history of numerous shipwrecks, during the 19th century, there were developments to lessen the dangers. By around 1830 there were three lighthouses in Anglesey, Skerries, South Stack and Point Lynas, and Penmon was completed in 1838. There was another one at Llanddwyn. Currently, remote control automatic lights are in operation at South Stack, Skerries, Penmon and Llanddwyn with a beacon at the Swellies and there is a lighthouse on Bardsey Island. South Stack has recently been reopened to the public after being closed for thirteen years. There is a new bridge for access and the building has been refurbished. It is well worthwhile going down the four hundred and nine steps to see the exhibition and the rock formation of the cliffs.

There were coastguards before the introduction of lifeboats, and volunteers who risked their lives to save others. In 1823 the *Alert,* bound for Liverpool from Dublin was shipwrecked on the West Mouse rock between the Skerries and the Anglesey coast. This tragedy, in which over a hundred lives were lost, deeply affected Frances Williams and her husband the Rev James Williams (1790-1872) the rector of Llanfair yng Nghornwy, curate of Llanfair Pwllgwyngyll and Penmynydd (1814-21), noted above. From then on they spared no effort in establishing, with the help of others, a Lifeboat Association for the island, the first in Wales. The first lifeboat was based near their home at Cemlyn in 1829, the second at Holyhead, then Rhoscolyn and Penmon; Llanddwyn was fifth and Moelfre sixth, and Rhosneigr in 1872. The Rev James Williams took an active part in rescue operations and in 1835 he rode on horseback into the stormy sea to throw a rope to a ship in distress off Cemaes enabling all hands to be saved. *Across the Straits* by J Kyffin Williams contains pictures of Thomas Williams mentioned above together with Frances and James Williams the great-grandparents of the artist. Kyffin Williams RA himself has concentrated on depicting the landscape of the area covered in this book as well as on portraits of the people who live here. There is an extensive exhibition of his work at Oriel Ynys Môn near Llangefni. The paintings reproduced in the book show that Frances Williams was also a gifted artist. In 1999 Kyffin will become Sir John Kyffin Williams.

At Rhoscolyn there is a memorial tablet to a brave dog, *Tyger*, which swam a number of times to rescue men from a sinking ship but died on its final attempt.

The lifeboats operating now are Holyhead, Moelfre, Trearddur Bay, Beaumaris, Porthdinllaen, Abersoch, Criccieth, Pwllheli, Barmouth, Conwy and Llandudno.

THE WRECK OF THE *'ROTHSAY CASTLE'*

As early as 1822 steam ships started sailing from Liverpool to Beaumaris and the Menai Straits and soon it was nearly a daily service between April and October.

The *Rothsay Castle* was one such passenger steamer that left Liverpool for North Wales on 17 August 1831, one hour later than her usual time. Not far out of Liverpool because of a rising gale the passengers tried to persuade the captain to turn back but he refused. Struggling ahead very slowly it was midnight before she was near Puffin Island and in imminent danger. Later she struck the Dutchman's Bank, part of Traeth Lafan, off Aberlleiniog and was battered by wind and wave. It is also alleged that the craft was not seaworthy and that the captain was drunk. About a 130 people were lost with only 23 surviving. The tragedy was the subject of a long poem in the Beaumaris Eisteddfod of 1832.

THE *ROYAL CHARTER*

During the heyday of trade and activity with the two new bridges across the Menai Straits opening up new horizons, two dramatic events occurred in the same year, 1859. One was the loss of the ship *The Royal Charter* off Moelfre, the other a large scale religious revival. The ship was a three-masted iron sailing clipper with a steam engine built in Flintshire in 1855 and she was on her way back to Liverpool from Melbourne laden with gold in her strong room and also carried by passengers on their persons. It was the night of 26 October when, in severe gales of hurricane force, a 133 ships were lost around the coasts of Britain. About 465 people lost their lives in the wreck of *The Royal Charter*; only 39, all men, survived. The vicar of Llanallgo, the Rev Stephen Roose Hughes and his brother, the Rev H R Hughes, arranged for the bodies to be carried into the church and before burial they did their best to secure some marks of identity. This thoughtful act helped them to inform and comfort the bereaved when answering over a thousand letters during the following weeks. There is a large chair made of timber from the Royal Charter in St Mary's church in Whitby, North Yorkshire. It was given in memory of the Rev William Scoresby a distinguished sailor and explorer who went out to Australia with the *Royal Charter* to test the effect of an iron ship on a compass that he was attempting to improve.

THE *HINDLEA*

By a strange coincidence, the *Hindlea*, a Cardiff cargo ship, was smashed to pieces on the rocks near Moelfre on 27 October 1959, exactly 100 years after the *Royal Charter* incident. The eight crew members were saved by the Moelfre lifeboat and the coxswain Richard Evans and crew were honoured.

THE *THETIS* AND WAR LOSSES

The loss of the submarine *Thetis* not far away near Traeth Bychan in 1939 was a more traumatic accident because those aboard were trapped for days. Ninety nine lives were lost. The submarine was raised, refitted and under the new name

Thunderbolt served during the Second World War and was lost.

In 1940 a steamer was lost off the Skerries having been attacked by a German aircraft and in 1945 a steamer was torpedoed off Anglesey. There had been many more losses during the Great War; nine ships were torpedoed off Anglesey mainly near Holyhead, and three off Bardsey and in Caernarfon Bay.

Velinheli, one of four ships owned by Dinorwig Quarry
Photo Derec Owen from original Mr Huntley Edwards

At **Moelfre** the lifeboat house is open to visitors during the summer and Anglesey Council have an interpretation centre nearby. This contains a lifeboat, artefacts from the *Royal Charter* and illustrations of the *Royal Charter* and the *Hindlea.*

Llandudno c. 1890

Conwy Castle and bridges

Page sponsored by Llandudno Town Council.

THE CONWY VALLEY AND LLANDUDNO

THE NAPLES OF THE NORTH

As a result of the establishment of the railway, Llandudno soon developed to be the queen of Welsh resorts. In the magazine *North Wales Lifestyle* edited by Bryn Havard and published by the North Wales Weekly News in the summer of 1988, a most interesting article about Victorian Llandudno, *Oh, They Did Like To Be Beside the Seaside* appeared. The author, unnamed, has pieced together the eleven day holiday of a family of four at the Evans Hotel in September 1895 the bill amounting to sixteen pounds one shilling. They enjoyed a trip around Anglesey with the Snowdon Steamship Company. From the pier, opened in 1877, there were excursions with the City of Dublin Packet Company down the Menai Straits to Caernarfon and to the Isle of Man. It was possible to go by train to Caernarfon and from there by coach to Llanberis in order to climb Snowdon. With regard to the popular bathing machines, which surprisingly were in use until 1958, these sheds on wheels were lowered into the sea so that the bathers could not 'indecently expose their persons'. It cost sixpence for forty minutes at the end of which the machine would be drawn up the beach by a horse. There was a Punch and Judy show started by a gypsy in 1864.

A short distance along the coast towards Colwyn Bay lies the smaller resort of Llandrillo yn Rhos or Rhos-on-Sea with the relaxing atmosphere of its promenade, delightful shops and the smallest church in Wales, measuring 15ft by 9ft (4.5m by 2.7m) dedicated to St Trillo. It illustrates the point that the early Celtic monks, Brythonic or Irish, were happy with a very small establishment, a tiny church usually made of wood, possibly stones where they were plentiful, for prayers, a well for drinking water and for baptizing, a graveyard for Christian burial when the converted were only a few, and a garden for vegetables. They were tough outdoor men who did manual work, walked a great deal and were strong boatmen. Such men were Seiriol of Penmon and Tudno who settled on the limestone of the Great Orme, saints in the tradition of Dewi, the patron saint of Wales.

THE EARLIEST MINES IN THE WORLD?

At the beginning of the 20th century the busy limestone quarry at Trwyn y Fuwch or the Little Orme provided work for a large number of men. Four thousand years earlier at the Great Orme men using bone, antlers and stone tools were mining for copper on a large scale reaching a depth of 300ft (91m). The Great Orme Bronze Age Copper Mines, now open to the public, is one of the most fascinating and educational attractions in the area. The headland itself is full of interest, the views of sea and mountains, wildlife, and prehistoric remains including Pen y Dinas, an ideal place for a defensive lookout. A good motor car road, the Marine Drive, round the headland, affords an excellent way to see the massive, limestone, awe-inspiring cliffs, so near to the straight, wide streets, the grand hotels on the promenade and the shops of the town. Owen Williams the Liverpool Welshman, who was invited by Edward Mostyn of Gloddaeth mansion to undertake the project, made an admirable job of planning the new town. The pier was opened in 1877 and the Happy Valley is from the same period. Ski Llandudno, an artificial ski slope and a 765yd (700m) toboggan run was opened more recently during the 1980's. There are four ways to the Orme summit, on foot, by car, by the tramway (the longest cable hauled tramway in Britain), or by cable car.

Other attractions include the Museum, Mostyn Art Gallery, the Rhos-on-Sea Harlequin Puppet Theatre which will delight the children and the Alice in Wonderland Centre. The original Alice Liddell, the daughter of an Oxford don who used to spend the summer holidays at West Shore during the 1860's, heard the stories told by a family friend Charles Lutwidge Dodgson. *Alice in Wonderland* was published under the *nom de plume* Lewis Carroll in 1865. A marble figure of Alice's white rabbit carved by a local stonemason Mr Forester was unveiled in 1933. The Welsh artist Hugh Hughes (1790-1863) was born in Llandudno and, like John Gibson the sculptor from Conwy, went to Liverpool as a boy. They were the same age and both were learning the skills of their art at the same time in that city.

Many visitors will have come to Llandudno to attend large gatherings at the new opera house cum conference centre and stayed at the hotels along the promenade without realizing that the above experiences and the West Shore beach sheltered from the North and East winds, were available so near at hand and that there are magnificent hotels such as Bodysgallen Hall on the outskirts. They should come back with the family.

CONWY - A WALLED TOWN

Wherever one turns there is a feature of interest in Conwy from the quay side with the smallest house in Britain to Aberconwy House a 14th century merchant's house and Plas Mawr, one of the best preserved Elizabethan town-houses in Britain. There is a Youth Hostel on the Sychnant Pass Road. The first Youth Hostel in Britain was opened in 1930 at Pennant Hall in the Conwy Valley, and incidentally the Youth Clubs in the area are listed under Holiday Accommodation in the Yellow Pages telephone directory. The well known sculptor John Gibson RA (1790-1866) was born at Gyffin near Conwy and lived there until he was ten. From Liverpool he went to London where he undertook prestigious commissions and then spent most of his life in Italy. His work was influenced by classical sculpture. There is a monument in the form of a bust in Conwy church which contains also a rood screen from 1500. Another son of Conwy who became well known was John Williams, Archbishop of York (1582-1650). He was descended from important Gwynedd families, went to Ruthin Grammar School, showed exceptional ability in languages and other fields and spent more than ten years at St John's College Cambridge. He was Archbishop of York when the Civil War broke out and as a fervent royalist repaired and held Conwy castle for a time until its former Governor, Sir John Owen returned and displaced him. Eventually he changed sides, joined the Parliamentarians and took part in an attack on Conwy castle. He was buried at Llandygai near Bangor where, also, is the grave of William Williams who developed the Penrhyn Quarry for Lord Penrhyn.

It is possible to walk the town walls built by the architect of the four great castles, James of St George for Edward I or Longshanks as he was called in the film *Braveheart* the story of the Scottish William Wallace. It was this river and this rock which served as a bulwark protecting fortress Gwynedd for **Llywelyn the Great**, whose monument stands in Lancaster Square, and his royal forefathers against invasions from England until the death of **Llywelyn the Last Prince** in 1282. Although the Welsh were fighting against overwhelming odds, even as late as November 1282 one English army trying to come over from Anglesey was routed in the Straits. The Archbishop of Canterbury, John Pecham, a Franciscan, tried to negotiate a surrender with an offer of land and a position for Llywelyn in England. Maurice Powicke in *The Thirteenth Century* wrote: 'Llywelyn in a brief and dignified letter, dismissed the *form* of submission as neither safe nor honourable and said that it had been heard with astonishment by all in council. No subjects of his, noble or freeman, would allow him, even if he wished, to consent to it. The reply of the Welsh was based on appeal to history and right. ... They repudiated the English offer of lands in England, for it came from men set on the Prince's disinheritance, so that they might have his lands in Wales. They would in no case recognize the exchange of Snowdon for land in England, a bargain which would require them to do homage to a stranger, of whose speech, manners and laws they were entirely ignorant'.

There was a popular misconception that Llywelyn ap Gruffudd was not of the same calibre as his grandfather, Llywelyn ap Iorwerth who has always been known as Llywelyn Fawr (The Great). Sir J E Lloyd, the great 20th century Welsh historian did not question the supremacy that history had bestowed upon him. More recent writers have emphasized the greatness of Llywelyn ap Gruffudd. David Stephenson in *The Last Prince of Wales* says: 'And in 1267 he had compelled Henry III of England to accept his greatness: Llywelyn was recognized as Prince of Wales - the only Welsh ruler ever to be so acknowledged by the English. Llywelyn's principal court at Aberffraw in Anglesey became the centre of the new realm of Wales for which the poets had clamoured'. In *Llywelyn ap Gruffudd* J Beverley Smith makes the point that the grandson's debt to the vision and achievement of his grandfather does not lessen his own feat.

CILMERI

It was an Englishman, Stanley Bligh who, in the first decade of the 20th century, at his own cost, had a memorial obelisk built to the memory of Llywelyn ap Gruffudd near Builth Wells. In 1956 another monument, the large stone of Penmaen-mawr granite from Gwynedd, his initial kingdom, and donated by Caernarfonshire, was erected. It is an impressive 15ft (4.5m) monolith on a grass mound, pointing upwards, firm and durable against all weathers, a fitting tribute. But it commemorates his death and downfall not his life.

Throughout the centuries there had not been a suitable individual memorial to him in Gwynedd, the kingdom that Gruffudd ap Cynan won back and kept, and the base from which Llywelyn Fawr, Prince of Aberffraw and Lord of Snowdonia, attained lordship over the other princes of Wales. The historian J Beverley Smith in 1986 published his authoritative biography of Llywelyn ap Gruffudd, the first and last Welsh Prince of all Wales. In 1267 at a ford on the Severn not far from Montgomery, Llywelyn paid homage to Henry III, the King of England, and in return the king conferred the rightful title Prince of Wales on him. Llywelyn had brothers and there had been attempts by the king to divide and rule by applying the Welsh legal custom of *gavelkind* i.e. equal division of lands among sons. Beverley Smith has made the case strongly that this did not apply to the royal line but that the prince would decide who was the appropriate heir. Llywelyn ap Gruffudd by his outstanding ability as a soldier and his powers of wise leadership was able to claim for himself the position of lord over the traditional home of the royal line and eventually as Prince of Wales. In the marble hall, of the Cardiff City Hall there is an important gallery of eleven 'Heroes of Wales' in white marble containing statues of Owain Glyndŵr and Llywelyn ap Gruffudd with right arm upraised suggesting a call to work and brave deeds. Surprisingly Llywelyn Fawr is not among the ten. The Heritage Centre and monument at Aberffraw in Anglesey commemorate the princes and in 1982 a monument to mark the seventh centenary of Llywelyn's death was unveiled at the Gwynedd County Council headquarters in Caernarfon. It consists of an aluminium sculpture on a massive slate slab donated by Penrhyn Quarry.

Llywelyn ap Gruffudd's decapitated body was buried at the Cistercian Abbey at Cwm Hir, five miles east of Rhaeadr and not far from Cilmeri, Radnorshire. Llywelyn ap Iorwerth and his son Dafydd were buried at Aberconwy and the body of Gruffudd ap Llywelyn was brought from London to be with them at the Cistercian Abbey.

Higher up the Conwy valley at Dolgarrog there was a catastrophe in 1925, when the dam at Llyn Eigiau broke and the rushing waters and large stones damaged or destroyed houses and sixteen people were drowned. The lakes Cowlyd and Eigiau are used to generate electricity for the national grid and the water supply for the valley. The aluminum plant, the only medium sized industry in this beautiful valley uses electricity from the national grid. Car access to the 'lake district' up in the hills to the west is from Talybont below, Trefriw above and from the famous Tŷ Hyll (Ugly House) near Betws-y-coed. The scenery is magnificent around the lakes Cowlyd, Crafnant and Geirionnydd. At Trefriw there are two visitor attractions, the Trefriw Wells Spa to rejuvenate the body and the spirit and Trefriw Woollen Mills where one can enjoy seeing the traditional weaving process and buy a genuine Welsh product that will last for years. One of the best poets of the 19th century, Evan Evans (Ieuan Glan Geirionydd), the author of some excellent hymns was born in Trefriw. After serving as a curate in various parishes he returned and was buried in the graveyard of Trefriw church in 1855.

Going up the valley we pass Llanrwst, the market town, noting the pleasant riverside recreation area and not forgetting to take a photograph of the old fashioned bridge. A few miles from Betws-y-coed there is another woollen mill at Penmachno in a picturesque wooded valley. Situated in the Wybrnant Valley, Tŷ Mawr was the birthplace of Bishop William Morgan who first translated the Bible into Welsh in 1588. When Bishop William Morgan from Penmachno, was translating the Bible into Welsh, in the years before 1588, he was putting into practice one of the great principles of Protestantism, making the word of God available to all who could read.

At the same time the conflict between the Catholic King Philip II of Spain and the Protestant Queen Elizabeth I of England culminated in the defeat of the Spanish Armada.

Acts of Parliament were in force requiring all the Queen's subjects to attend the Anglican parish church and most of them conformed, outwardly at least. Many of the clergy like William Morgan were enthusiastic Protestants. But some of the gentry in North West Wales such as the Owen family of Plas Du and others in Llŷn, and the Pugh family in Penrhyn Creuddyn near Llandudno were staunch Catholics. Many educated young men with strong convictions fled to the continent to educate young priests as missionaries and in order to publish Catholic literature.

Owen Lewis (1533-95) born in Llangadwaladr in Anglesey assisted in setting up the college for this purpose at Douai near Calais in 1568. Later he became a very influential figure in the Vatican. Gruffydd Robert (1522-1610) was probably born in Caernarfonshire and was Archdeacon of Anglesey for a short period while Queen Mary was alive. He left and held posts in Rome and Milan. Morys Clynnog (1525-81) from Clynnog Fawr in Caernarfonshire was Bishop-elect of Bangor but took the same course and was in Rome in 1561. Far away from home these men published Welsh books to be distributed secretly in Wales.

William Davies from near Colwyn Bay and Robert Gwynn came back as missionaries and under the protection of Robert ap Hugh of Penrhyn Creuddyn (Llandudno) they held services in secret and set up a printing press. To avoid arrest and confiscation this had to be moved to a cave on the Little Orme but under further persecution in 1587 they fled but carried on with their desperate mission. William Davies was imprisoned for a long time and eventually hanged, drawn and quartered at Beaumaris in July 1593.

The oldest Christian gravestone in Wales dating from 500 AD which was found in this area at Penmachno commemorates a man whose name was *Cantiorix* and who is described as *Venedotis Cives* (a Citizen of Gwynedd). Nearby, only 1 mile (1.6km) from **Llanrwst** stands the carefully restored Tudor mansion, Gwydir Castle, with the eye-catching colourful peacocks strutting around on the lawns or along the walls. This was the home of the very influential Wynn family whose history was written by the land-grabbing tyrant Sir John (1553-1627). Attached to the parish church of Llanrwst is the most attractive Capel Gwydir built by Sir Richard Wynn in 1634 the design of which is attributed to Inigo Jones (1573-1652). The narrow hump-backed bridge with its central arch and smaller ones on each side, referred to above, is also attributed to the same architect but that was not accepted by Bob Owen the local historian from Croesor. Part of the large stone coffin of Llywelyn Fawr, moved from Maenan Abbey during the dissolution, is now in this chapel. This building is not to be confused with the very ornate private chapel also built by Sir Richard situated a little higher up from the house Gwydir Uchaf which is not far from Gwydir Castle. Plas Isaf, the home of William Salesbury (1520?-1584?) who first translated the New Testament into Welsh before William Morgan's Bible, was in Llanrwst. The great Renaissance scholar was assisted by another son of Dyffryn Conwy, Bishop Richard Davies from Gyffin in the translation of the New Testament and the Prayer Book.

These Protestant efforts saw their culmination in William Morgan's masterpiece of 1588 which in time became the strongest unifying cultural force that Wales has experienced. Its dignified language, understood throughout Wales when heard in church, became a pattern for prose.

Where your treasure is there will your heart be also - St Mathew

INIGO JONES (1573-1652)

Inigo Jones was born in London of a Roman Catholic family. Having shown ability in drawing, designing and landscape painting he was able, with patronage, to spend some time in Italy whose buildings, theatres and works of art had a lasting influence on his work. He was an architect to Kings James I and Charles I, classed with Sir Christopher Wren, and largely responsible for a revolution in English building. He was the designer of many famous buildings such as the Banqueting Hall at Westminster, the Royal Naval College at Greenwich and the Queen's House opposite. His family was associated with a coat of arms borne by a Denbighshire family. It is possible that he did some work for Sir Richard Wynn of Gwydir. Sir Richard accompanied Prince Charles to Spain to woo Princess Henrietta Maria who as Queen had the house at Greenwich built by Inigo Jones. Sir Richard held the post of Treasurer to the Queen's household when Charles became King.

THE RIVER CONWY

The Conwy, the longest river in this part of North Wales, has been described by Sir J E Lloyd the historian as a 'moat drawn by nature for the defence of the Snowdonian fastnesses'. The same author quotes Edmund Spencer:

> Conway, which out of his streame doth send
> Plenty of pearles to deck his dames withall.

The fresh water pearl fishery was above Trefriw. The Conwy rises in Llyn Conwy in the mountains above Cwm Penmachno, goes past Ysbyty Ifan, turns sharply to the left to Conwy Falls and Fairy Glen. The Lledr joins it and the Llugwy at Betws-y-coed and then flowing more slowly on level ground it goes north being navigable from Trefriw down to the estuary. As well as being essential for small ships and boats carrying freight, as were the Glaslyn and Dwyryd estuaries, pleasure trips up the Conwy were very popular.

Of all the attractions of the lovely Conwy Valley the jewel in the crown must be the National Trust's **Bodnant Garden** on the east side of the valley near Talycafn, the home of a marvellous collection of azaleas and rhododendrons, magnolias and camellias. This garden, in part formal but mostly merging naturally into wooded slopes down to the river, lingers in the memory like the scent of the azaleas. The spectacular Laburnum Arch is at its best in late May and early June. It was originally set out in 1875. In 1920 F C Puddle became head gardener and since then two other artists, his son Charles and now Martin his grandson have followed in his footsteps. The author Jan Morris has called it 'one of the supreme gardens of the world'.

Near the road on the A470 between Betws-y-coed and Blaenau Ffestiniog, stands

Dolwyddelan Castle, a strong square building with the mountains behind it. Like Dolbadarn castle in Llanberis it was built by the native princes of Wales before Edward built the great fortresses to suppress the Welsh.

Dolwyddelan Castle *Gwynedd County Council*

Llywelyn ap Iorwerth
Conwy
Gwynedd County Council

Monument to Last Prince
Caernarfon
Gwynedd County Council

MENAI BRIDGE - INTERNATIONAL PORT

The outstanding entrepreneurs of Menai Bridge during the time of Thomas Hughes the tailor were the Davies family of Treborth. The father John Davies from Llangefni was a business man. John his son, taking advantage of the steamship trade from Liverpool to Menai Bridge developed a mainly timber and iron business and they acquired their own ships during 1845-7, the *Enterprise, Agnes, Chieftain, Courtenay and Oregon* all just over 1000 tons. Their ships would sail from Menai Bridge to New York, Quebec and New Orleans, taking emigrants out and bringing back flour and timber. The most famous son was Richard, a Methodist and Liberal who was elected MP for Anglesey in 1868, Sir Richard Bulkeley supporting his candidature. This was the first time for a man not from the landowning aristocracy to represent the island. Many poor people were helped by this family by being given free flour.

When you open the sack that is the hour
To think ahead and save the flour.

(Welsh proverb)

BEAUMARIS - AFTER 700 YEARS

Beaumaris, about 7 miles (11km) North East of Llanfair, on the edge of the Menai Straits facing the mountains above Aber, Llanfairfechan and Penmaen-mawr is the most attractive and interesting town in Anglesey. The winding road from Porthaethwy (Menai Bridge) affords glimpses of the mainland and Bangor pier on the right hand side. As the road approaches Beaumaris after Gallows Point the bay comes into view with the different coloured yachts and boats riding at anchor when the tide is in. The French name given to the site of the castle by the Normans was 'beau marais', beautiful marsh, the former Welsh name of the little port being 'Porth Wygyr'. Built between 1295 and 1298 by Edward I the castle complements the great fortress at Caernarfon at the other, western, end of the Menai Straits, and Conwy on the west side of the River Conwy, each one having access to the sea and enabling the conqueror to control the supply of corn to Snowdonia. Because of its concentric plan, a castle within a castle, Beaumaris is considered unique. These gigantic strongholds against the rural setting of North Wales remain to show the tough resistance put up by the Welsh. A massive workforce was involved in the building of Beaumaris castle, a 1,000 labourers, 400 skilled craftsmen and 200 carters, many of them brought from far afield in England. The stones for Beaumaris and Caernarfon came largely from Penmon. An interesting feature of the castle, not apparent today, is that the moat was connected to the sea so that ships could come alongside the walls. Work on the construction of Caernarfon and Conwy and the repairing of Criccieth castle was started in 1283 and in the case of Caernarfon continued until 1321.

ENGLISH BOROUGHS ESTABLISHED

Before the new town of Beaumaris, outside the castle, but within its town walls, received its charter in 1296 similar boroughs were established in Caernarfon, Conwy and Criccieth, the first two receiving their charters in 1284 and Criccieth in 1285, charters which incorporated the rights and privileges of the burgesses. In 1355 Pwllheli and Nefyn also were awarded charters. As was the case with Beaumaris, at Conwy, Caernarfon and Criccieth the burgesses were English people brought in while the Welsh were kept out. Castle Street in Beaumaris is straight from one end of the town to the other while the streets in Caernarfon and Conwy are also straight and cross at right angles. This was so when the towns were within the boundary walls. Markets and fairs providing an opportunity for the Welsh to conduct business with the residents were held outside the walls. The burgesses were given land, taken from the Welsh, for crops and animals, rent-free for ten years and the right to be tried according to English law, the jury being English people.

THE TOWN

The courthouse dating from 1614 is open to visitors and is still used symbolically on occasions as a court of law. Inside, a humorous touch is the picture of a cow, one farmer pulling at its horns and another at its tail while in the middle there is a third person milking it, the solicitor. The old Grammar School nearby was founded in 1603 by David Hughes originally from Llantrisant in Anglesey and then the steward of Woodrising in Norfolk.

The Museum of Childhood opposite the castle entrance, the gaol, opened in 1829, the green and the pier, are popular tourist attractions. The most attractive building is the Tudor Rose shop, black and white, of oak and lath and plaster construction, from about 1400. In the porch of the Church of St Mary and St Nicholas is the stone coffin of Siwan (Joan), the wife of Llywelyn the Great and natural or illegitimate daughter of King John of England, who was buried at the Franciscan friary at Llanfaes. Joan was her father's favourite daughter. In *The Historic Gardens of Wales* (Cadw HMSO 1992) there is a picture of 'the tomb of Princess Joan at Baron Hill'. At the suppression of the friary at Llan-faes under Henry VIII, the coffin was removed to Baron Hill and probably in the 18th century, following the antiquarian fashion, 'Lord Bulkeley built a temple in which he placed the coffin of Princess Joan'. Nothing remains of the mansion of Baron Hill, home of the Bulkeley family, one of the most powerful landowners in Wales for centuries. The Baron

Hill papers are kept in the library of University of Wales, Bangor.

A recent effective addition to the attractions of Beaumaris is the horse-drawn vehicle pulled by a shire horse. Similar tourist rides are available also at Betws-y-coed while there is a new shire horse centre at Hendre near Penrhyn Castle. Every seven years the ceremony of Beating the Bounds, that is, marking the boundary of the town takes place. The traditional walk led by the Mayor and Town Council has been kept up since 1296 and involves one or two climbing over the roof of a farmhouse and walking through the water under Pont y Brenin in Llangoed.

LLAN-FAES

The port of the town of Llan-faes, a very important administrative centre in the Early Middle Ages, was very busy. Between 1280 and 1290 the annual number of ships calling there jumped from thirty to eighty. The trade included a herring fishery, a ferry, ships carrying agricultural products and general cargo and it was the main centre for importing wine from France. Apart from the port about half a mile inland was the town with all its various trades and fairs, the church and above all the king's court. Of the commercial centres in Gwynedd, Caernarfon, Nefyn, Pwllheli and Tywyn, Llan-faes was the most important. By the time Llywelyn Fawr of Gwynedd was recognized as ruler of all Wales his main court was at Aberffraw. Aber near Bangor was also important and there were others such as Rhosyr and Llan-faes where the king held court. Although Llywelyn had paid homage to the king of England under the feudal system and is called prince the homage was in name only and he was 'king' in his own domain.

Early in the 13th century Prince Llywelyn ap Iorwerth of the Gwynedd royal line became the king and overlord of Gwynedd. Being a powerful soldier, diplomat and politician he was able to get all of Wales under his control as was his grandson Llywelyn ap Gruffudd called Llywelyn the Last Prince. When Llywelyn Fawr's wife Siwan (Joan) died in 1237 she was buried at Llan-faes and Llywelyn in her memory made it possible for the followers of St Francis to establish a friary between the town and the port. It was the first such establishment in Wales. In this way rulers were able to help religious orders by being benefactors and showing official approval and in return had masses said for the souls of the departed and found them a help in providing stability in the kingdom. Eleanor de Montfort, the wife of Llywelyn the Last was buried there also.

SAINT FRANCIS OF ASSISI

Francis the son of a rich merchant from Umbria, a little to the North of Rome, had a dramatic conversion after which he renounced family and riches and followed in the footsteps of Jesus Christ in a very strict way. He dedicated his life to teaching and preaching and although his emphasis on absolute poverty and setting an example was in contrast to the church he did secure papal support. Because of his saintliness he is said to have received the marks of the stigmata or scars corresponding to the marks of the nails and spear on the body of Jesus at the Crucifixion. His many followers became known as the grey friars. The remarkable fact is that having decided to establish outposts beyond Italy in 1217 and arriving in England in 1224, only thirteen years later they were established at Llan-faes in Anglesey. Because of their work in attending to the sick and dying they were nearly wiped out in Wales at the time of the Black Death. They relied entirely on begging for sustenance and as the order could not own property, their home or friary belonged to their benefactor. Rich and noble people were buried in the churchyard of the Friary including Lord Clifford and other lords and knights and the son of the King of Denmark. Whereas Llywelyn had founded the house and church for the Franciscan friars the king of England Henry VIII was responsible for their disintegration in 1538. When Llywelyn died in 1240 he was buried at the Cistercian monastery of Aberconwy which he had founded. After the conquest by Edward I, in 1283 the monastery was destroyed and the castle built over Llywelyn's resting place. The monks were moved to Maenan and with them the coffin of Llywelyn which now rests in Capel Gwydir, Llanrwst. But in Lancaster Square, Conwy, stands proudly a monument by the sculptor E O Griffiths, not large, but showing Llywelyn resplendent with his shield and long sword and a crown on his head.

LLAN-FAES - FRYARS - SAUNDERS ROE

At the beginning of the 20th century there was a mansion in the quiet grounds at Llan-faes on the site of the Franciscan Friary. During the Second World War the grounds of this country house were completely transformed when the Isle of Wight aircraft and boat company, Saunders Roe Ltd located the major part of its activities on the site. With its boundary walls skirting the Menai Straits it was an ideal situation.

From 1940 arrangements were made to accommodate design and drawing office staff at Fryars and subsequently a slipway and hangars or workshops were built. Although a number of flying boats including Shetlands, Coronados, Kingfishers and Sunderlands were seen at Fryars by far the most important were the Catalinas. The work, for which a local workforce was recruited with great success, was adapting the Catalinas from the USA. They were used by the air force for anti-submarine patrols. At first, during 1941, the seaplanes were delivered to Greenock on the Clyde and flown from there to Beaumaris. In November 1942 the first one direct from Bermuda arrived while in 1943 Catalinas built by Boeing in Canada arrived in Fryars.

This adaptation and conversion work came to an end in 1945 and the factory became known as Saunders Engineering and Shipyard Company. Pontoons or aluminium parts for bridges were built and later, buses which were exported worldwide. Early in the fifties exciting work was done in the construction of minesweepers, airborne lifeboats, fast patrol boats and light alloy assault boats. This necessitated building a new launching slipway. Later, refuse collecting vehicles were made at the factory.

PENMON

About 3 miles (4.8km) to the North East along the coast in tranquil serenity lies Penmon church and priory within surrounding limestone walls. The highest point is the pyramidal slab roof above the 12th century church with its thick, strong Norman arches. Above green fields sloping gently to the sea, the monastic buildings, the dovecote from about 1600, the well, the quiet waters of the fishing pond amid the trees, together recreate the atmosphere of another age. The high walls in the vicinity were the boundaries of a deer park on Baron Hill land.

SAINT SEIRIOL

In the 6th century a tiny church and cell were built for the monk Seiriol by his brother Cynlas. They were both descendants of Cunedda, a royal warrior who, it is claimed, came early in the 5th century from what is now Southern Scotland and settled in the vicinity of the strategic Menai Straits. The Brythonic language was common to the people of Northern Britain as well as Wales and the Romanized compatriots were able jointly to regain most of Gwynedd from the Irish settlers.

When Seiriol's establishment at Penmon and Ynys Seiriol (Puffin Island) developed it became a Celtic 'clas' which was a primitive monastery. There was a simple church together with wattle and daub huts which served as individual living quarters for the monks. The head of the community was the abbot. Seiriol was also the chief saint of the Dwygyfylchi district in Arfon with a cell or chapel at Penmaenmawr across the Straits from Penmon. The same is true with regard to Cybi whose chief establishment was at Caergybi (Holyhead) but is associated with Llangybi not far from Porthmadog. The highly developed church and monastic buildings, the stone walls of which we see today in Penmon, were built during the 12th and 13th centuries with the help of the kings Owain Gwynedd and Llywelyn the Great. By the 13th century Penmon had developed into a priory of the order of St Augustine.

In 1537 the secluded devotional life of the monks came to an abrupt end. By order of King Henry VIII the priory was closed, the valuables plundered and the land transferred to the Bulkeley family.

Less than 1 mile (1km) further on is the pleasant promontory Trwyn Du and Ynys Seiriol formerly Ynys Lannog (Puffin Island).

NORSEMEN IN THE IRISH SEA

Of the Norsemen or Vikings it was the men of Norway who raided the Western Isles of Scotland, Ireland and Wales around 1,000 AD. It was they who established Dublin during the 9th century. In our area their influence remains in the place-names Anglesey (*Ongull*, personal name and *-ey*, island as in Orkney), Priestholm (Puffin Island), Orme near Llandudno and the Skerries off Holyhead. The Norse elements are *ey* and *holm*, island; *orme*, serpent; *prest*, priest and *sker*, rock.

2,000 ANGLESEY MEN CAPTURED AND SOLD AS SLAVES.

Despite Gwynedd's tradition of brave warrior kings in the Early Middle Ages Anglesey must have been very vulnerable in 987. It is recorded that in that year the Norsemen or Vikings captured two thousand of the island's men to be sold as slaves. One wonders where they all landed up. Taking 175,000 as a rough indication of the population of the whole of Wales we begin to understand the extent of the tragedy.

GRUFFUDD AP CYNAN - HALF WELSH HALF VIKING

Because of the internal strife between rivals within Wales during the second half of the 11th century, one Welsh leader, Cynan, who had a strong claim to the kingdom of Gwynedd had fled to Ireland. There he married a princess, the daughter of the Norse king of Dublin. Their son Gruffudd ap Cynan was born in 1055 and brought up outside Dublin. Cynan was probably killed in battle in Snowdonia in 1063. By 1094, Gruffudd, half Welsh half Norse, had regained the kingdom of Gwynedd. He was able to do this with the help of Vikings who had by that time become Christians, that is around 1075-1098.

THE NORMAN INVADERS

The Vikings occupied Normandy and later as Normans invaded England. Within six years of 1066 the Norman William had conquered England and he reigned until 1087. From 1087 until 1100 he was followed by his son William Rufus and from 1100 until 1135 by Henry I, William Rufus's brother. On the frontier between England and Wales they gave their Norman friends a free hand to try to control the Welsh. During the years after 1066 these were; Earl William of Hereford, Earl

Roger of Shrewsbury and Earl Hugh (the fat) of Chester. They were continually trying to gain the upper hand and claim new territories. Gruffudd ap Cynan, the king of Gwynedd was the leader of Welsh resistance to these frontier barons. Not only Vikings but Irish and Manx soldiers helped Gruffudd to regain Gwynedd in 1094 after many unsuccessful attempts.

ABERLLEINIOG

Aberlleiniog, about 9 miles (14km) from Llanfair Pwllgwyngyll, is between Llanfaes and Penmon. One of the decisive victories of Gruffudd's campaign against Hugh of Chester was the routing of the garrison of the wooden motte and bailey castle at Aberlleiniog near Llangoed at the mouth of the Menai in 1094. Because of Anglesey's proximity to Ireland and the involvement of the Norsemen, fighting from ships and boats and skirmishes on the coast were features of his campaigns. After his success at Aberlleiniog he went on to take many other castles. He was eventually able to rule his kingdom for nearly forty years setting a fine example to succeeding kings of Gwynedd. The mound, with the ruins of the castle walls built of stone at a later date, is still to be seen together with a mound of earth by the shore which was a lookout point.

THE BATTLE OF ABERLLEINIOG

In 1098 the Normans wanted revenge. Hugh Lupus of Chester and Hugh, Earl of Shrewsbury joined forces to attack North Wales by land and sea. They invaded Anglesey and committed savage barbarities on the island. But fortunately for the Welsh the fleet of Magnus Barefoot the King of Norway was on the Irish Sea not far away and, deciding to inspect the island, they were opposed by the Normans. The accurate Norse archers killed and wounded many of the armoured Norman knights among them Hugh of Shrewsbury who was pierced in his eye. When the Normans left in disarray Gruffudd ap Cynan was able to regain control of his kingdom. He died in 1137, an old man of eighty two, and was buried to the left of the altar in Bangor cathedral.

LIMESTONE AND MARBLE

Along the coast from Penmon to Llanddona there used to be a number of quarries, some such as Parc and Y Fedw being worked in the 19th century and others continuing until the 20th century. Some large blocks remaining under the cliffs at Y Fedw suggest that this was one source of stone for the construction of the Menai Bridges and large buildings. The geology of Anglesey is varied and interesting. In this South Eastern part, limestone predominates although some red gritstone was obtained from Dinmor Park to refurbish Beaumaris church during the 1950's.

Flagstaff Quarry Penmon, Mr George Fingland in front of large stone c. 1910
Courtesy Mrs S Jeffs

Saunders Roe Fryars Bay
Courtesy Mr Stops

Llangoed Village c. 1910

PENMON MARBLE QUARRY

The first quarry on the left hand side, inside the deer park walls, just before the entrance to Penmon Priory, called in Welsh 'chwarel parc', has been derelict for most of this century. An example of the dressed stone may be seen on the right hand side of the road in the form of a gateway with Penmon Marble Quarry 1877 inscribed on the lintel. On the shore the stonework of the pier remains as well as the walls of sheds which contained cutting and possibly polishing equipment. The chimney stack for the steam power remains close by. There is a derelict building on private property within the quarry and there is a narrow rail track that runs under the road to the sheds and pier. Some regular blocks of grey stone can be seen and there is some brown rock on the quarry face. The marble when polished is grey, one example in the form of a round pillar to be seen in the chemist's shop in Beaumaris. It is claimed that it has been used for decorative purposes also in the marble church at Bodelwyddan and in Birmingham Town Hall.

Marble is defined as a metamorphosed limestone in which the calcite has been recrystallized. The crystal faces on a freshly broken surface sparkle like fine sugar. Pure marble is white but impurities provide colour, the Irish green Connemara variety being most attractive. Edward Greenly in his book on the geology of Anglesey refers to the Rhoscolyn marble, a beautiful green and white rock and has high praise for that of Bodwrog, parts of which are snow white while other parts have green and purplish tints. Mrs E A Williams in her excellent book about 19th century Anglesey draws attention to the marble of Maes Mawr quarry Llanfechell, a green stone, and reveals that George Bullock (d.1826), a cabinet maker and designer, made a beautiful table of this *verd antique,* as the marble from Italy was called, for Napoleon's residence in exile at St Helena. According to Celia and Ian Skidmore in *Anglesey Rambles* Bullock who was held in high esteem by antique specialists used Penmon and Llanfechell marble extensively in his furniture. The nearest place to Llanfair Pwllgwyngyll where the green Mona marble could be seen, in panels on chimney pieces, was at Plas Rhianfa, Llandegfan, a large house overlooking the Straits, now converted into flats.
'Able was I ere I saw Elba'. Napoleon Bonaparte. (Try going back).

BECYN (FLAGSTAFF) QUARRY

At the beginning of the 20th century Flagstaff Quarry, in Welsh 'Y Becyn' probably from the English 'beacon' was in operation as was Carreg Onnen near Llanddona. The owners of Y Becyn was a firm called Baird and Dalmellington and the manager was a Scotsman, George Fingland, who came to Penmon when he was twenty one years of age and who learned Welsh thoroughly. After 1818 stone for the Menai Suspension Bridge was quarried in Penmon and a quay built so that barges could carry the stone to Porthaethwy. It is not clear which quarry or quarries supplied this stone since the above mentioned as well as Sychnant (Dinmor) were possible sources. Greenly the geologist notes that the heavy blocks for the two Menai Bridges came from Castell Mawr and other quarries in Red Wharf Bay.

DINMOOR QUARRY - BIRKENHEAD - LIVERPOOL

From 1928 stone from this quarry in Penmon and from the neighbouring Carreg Onnen, Anglesey, was instrumental in keeping the great docks of Liverpool open for big ships while granite from Penmaen-mawr was used to build important buildings in Liverpool and for the Mersey tunnels.

The River Mersey rises in Cheshire and from its source to Liverpool is 56 miles (90km) long. Towards the end of the 19th century ships were increasing in draught and for many years, because of silting, large scale dredging was carried out to keep the channel open. By 1912 it was becoming clear that some other method of deepening and maintaining the channels was needed. After much discussion and many experiments with models it was decided to proceed with a scheme of training walls or revetment. The principle was to lay down ridges of stone or artificial reefs on the river bed, thus constraining the river and the tide and clearing the channel of sand and mud. The stone was brought from North Wales quarries in hopper barges and dumped in a planned way. In 1928 David Evans of Birkenhead was able to secure an order for 1,000,000 tons of stone from the Mersey Docks and Harbour Board. In 1927 he had bought the Dinmor Park Quarry in a derelict state. Sir Richard Williams-Bulkeley was the ground landlord to whom the royalties were paid.

LOCAL BOY MAKES GOOD

David Evans, born in 1870, was brought up in Cerrig Duon a smallholding very near to the Dinmor Park Quarry. An uncle had a coal delivery business in Birkenhead. Two older brothers, Richard and John had gone to Birkenhead and built up a haulage business being team owners and contractors in Wallasey. At one time they had ninety horses.

After attending the Penmon National School, when he was fifteen David also went to Birkenhead and worked in a grocer's shop for two years. After another four years working for his brothers he started team-owning and contracting on his own account. He was still only twenty one. In 1897 he sold his business and concentrated on buying land and building houses. The first venture was to buy a large house and land in Wallasey. This house which was to be demolished belonged to Sir John Tobin. David Evans built about a hundred houses on the land, continued

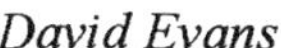

David Evans

Lord Evans of Claughton

Mr and Mrs John Cynlais Evans

Pier at Sychnant Quarry Penmon

Photos courtesy of Lady Evans of Claughton.

to buy land in Birkenhead and built lots of a hundred and more houses, shops and a cinema. In all he built around two thousand properties so that land developed near Bidston Hill was called David's City by the local Welsh people. He established the firm Messrs Evans, Jones and Evans and later opened an office in Hamilton Square under the name David Evans and Foster. Near Birkenhead Park the roads bearing the names of flowers, Daffodil, Primrose, Iris and so on were built by David Evans. He was proud of the fact that he had the same foremen and men working for him for thirty years, many of them from the Penmon and Llangoed area. He built some houses in those two villages to improve the housing in his home area.

In the venture of buying and setting up the quarry he was a great benefactor to his home part of Anglesey. After the general strike of 1926 and during the depression of the thirties he was able to provide employment for over two hundred men, on occasions at great cost to himself. He was a member of Birkenhead Town Council for three years and for a period represented his home village on Anglesey County Council and served as High Sheriff of Anglesey in 1933.

Some parts of this book may seem parochial but the local example is usually representative. For example the pictures of a carpenter's workshop developing into a bicycle shop and then into a garage; the Dinsylwy hill-fort and the Tŷ Mawr Cromlech. In the same way the story of the supplying of stones for the Liverpool Dock Board illustrates what happened in other quarries in the area. The fairly detailed story of David Evans from Penmon building houses in Birkenhead, similarly, gives a glimpse of the same activity by other builders from North West Wales such as Mr William Jones from the Llannerch-y-medd district building in Bootle, Liverpool. After leaving Anglesey during the 1860's he built houses in Toxteth and Everton and then concentrated on the growing Bootle. Known in Bootle as 'Klondyke' Jones he built the following streets: Gower, Holywell, Denbigh, Bala and Anglesey. Being a strict teetotaller himself he refused to allow development for public houses. He became High Sheriff of Anglesey and in 1886 the first Welsh speaking Mayor of Bootle. He died in 1918.

BIRKENHEAD

During the First World War the National Eisteddfod of 1917 was held in Birkenhead Park. It was the most memorable of all because the chair-winning poet, Hedd Wyn, from Trawsfynydd had been killed a few weeks earlier in Belgium. The chair known as Y Gadair Ddu (The Black Chair) because it was draped in black was given by David Evans. There is sombre irony in the fact that the craftsman who made the chair was a Belgian refugee Mons Van Fleteren who had settled in Birkenhead. The ornately decorated chair has a Celtic cross on the panel together with other Celtic motifs and dragons on the arms. David Evans later gave a red coloured stone to commemorate the site of the Eisteddfod in Birkenhead Park.

His two homes were called Cynlais, one in Penmon and the other in Shrewsbury Road, Birkenhead. His eldest son was John Cynlais Evans who in a remarkable turn-around came to live in Llanfair Pwllgwyngyll during the 1950's, bought fields opposite the David Hughes School in Menai Bridge and built a large estate of houses, Cae Tros Lôn. Griffith Evans his son, was prominent in local government in Birkenhead and was a Liberal Parliamentary Candidate twice. He was honoured for his work by being made Lord Evans of Claughton.

NEWBOROUGH - LLYS RHOSYR

There is a field near the parish church of St Peter called Cae Llys (Court Field), the name indicating some historical significance. There is also documentary evidence that an important court belonging to the princes of Gwynedd was situated at Rhosfair, later Rhosyr, near Newborough. Llywelyn ap Iorwerth wrote from there in 1237. The church has a font and gravestones from the 12th century.

The new borough was established by the Normans in 1303 on extensive manorial lands. The sand dunes on the south west coast around Aberffraw and Newborough show the significant effect of sand being blown inland by the prevailing wind over the centuries but it is recorded that there was a particularly violent storm in 1331 covering a very large area including the Rhosyr lands in deep sand. The great catastrophe causing the destruction of dwellings and agricultural land at the time has proved invaluable from an archaeological point of view. Excavations started by the Gwynedd Archaeological Trust in 1992 and continuing, have exposed the foundation walls of a timber hall and other buildings. The evidence from artefacts found indicate that the site was abandoned early in the 14th century. The site is unique in Wales and of international significance. In the words of the Trust: 'The pattern of government was eclipsed with the English conquest. Now for the first time we have the opportunity to flesh out the theory with real detail on the number, disposition, character, function, building materials, structural form and chronology of a Welsh Llys'.

LLANDDWYN

Llanddwyn beach with its miles of flat sand sheltered from the east wind is now very popular. The marram grass that grows on the dunes used to be the basis of a local industry including basket work and the production of mats and rick covers. An attempt being made to revive this old country craft deserves support. On the northern edge of the beach, at the tip of a promontory which becomes an island at high tide there is an automatically operated lighthouse.

It is to another landmark that romantic young people make their way, the few remains of the church, with a well nearby, of St Dwyn or Dwynwen, (the blessed Dwyn) the Welsh patron saint of lovers. Dwynwen, the beautiful daughter of Brychan Brycheiniog, was in love with a young prince, Maelon, but her father disapproved. In her disappointment and sadness she left home and sought solace in the contemplative life on this typically remote corner of a distant island. The date celebrated is 25 January.

ABERFFRAW

Aberffraw on the west coast of Anglesey was during the Middle Ages the main court of the princes of Gwynedd and according to the Mabinogion it was where the wedding feast of Branwen and Matholwch was held. There is no trace of the palace which would have been of timber construction but Anglesey Council has built a heritage centre as a memorial called Llys Llywelyn. Outside there is a sculpture in stone and slate *Y Tywysogion* (The Princes) by the writer and sculptor Jonah Jones.

Within walking distance of Aberffraw lies Porth Cwyfan and a short distance from the shore and accessible at low tide the small island Ynys Cwyfan, the rock on which the 12th century church has been built. The original monk's cell from the 6th century would have been a typical Celtic settlement. There is a significant connection with Ireland in that the Irish saint who founded it is associated also with the famous Glendalough in Wicklow.

The village and church of **Llangadwaladr** are within two miles of Aberffraw. Inside the church there is an important gravestone, that of Cadfan who died in 625 AD. The Latin inscription reads: '*Catamanus rex sapientissimus opinatissimus omnium regum*', King Cadfan, the wisest and most praiseworthy of all the kings.

HOLYHEAD

Apart from the major port of Holyhead the extent of the harbour improvements during the 19th century can be judged today at Porthmadog, Caernarfon, Port Dinorwig, Porth Penrhyn and Porth Amlwch. To enable shipping companies in Liverpool to receive information a relay semaphore system was introduced in 1825 by the Mersey Docks and Harbour Board. The stations were on Holyhead Mountain, Llanrhyddlad, Llaneilian, Bodafon, Puffin Island, the Great Orme and others about eight miles apart to Liverpool. With experience it developed into a very efficient communications system. Thomas Jackson in his *Visitor's Guide to*

Holyhead described the contraption: 'The Telegraph consists of two vertical arms, movable on pivots, at a sufficient distance from each other to prevent any confusion in the working'.

During the first decades of the 19th century major improvements were made to Holyhead. Before any developments its significance was that it was on the route of the Irish Mail where the 'packet' or state papers were taken aboard ship. It was also possible for private persons to avail themselves of the facility. In 1809 South Stack lighthouse was completed and by 1824 the harbour had been improved. In *Holyhead, the Story of a Port* D Lloyd Hughes and Dorothy M Williams have traced the developments of the old sea and railway town with clarity and affection. The first major step was to join Salt Island to Holy Island, build the Admiralty Pier to the east from Salt Island and the Government dry or graving dock for ship maintenance protected by the South Pier. On the Salt Island pier the new Customs House and Harbour Office were built. Work on the breakwater started in 1845 laying down railtracks to the Holyhead Mountain quarry. Many thousands of tons of stones were carried in trucks drawn by horse and locomotive to form this long artificial reef stretching far out northwards and then to the east. It was necessary to have large heavy stones and the supply from the mountain was supplemented with limestone from Moelfre. Steady improvements were at the same time made to the station, the engine sheds and cattle yards necessitating a large workforce which in its turn required more and better houses, shops, public houses and chapels. The Five Sisters, the public houses opposite the station called the Blossoms, Globe, Sydney, Dublin Packet and Holland were well known. It is not surprising that there were many more pubs in this cosmopolitan port. But there was another side to the life of Holyhead, the chapels. In an eloquent tribute, this is how David Lloyd Hughes wrote: 'These men (the preachers) were such potent forces in the life of the community that it is important to put them in the right perspective if one is to understand the great days of Nonconformity in Holyhead. In the first place they should not be dismissed as mob orators charming an illiterate people; great preachers were men of outstanding intellectual ability who would have adorned many professions in another age. In their day the climate of life was religious and the majority of talented boys would not wish to aspire to any other calling; it must also be admitted that it was a glamorous calling, for all preachers were admired and the outstanding ones were idolized on a national scale. It must also be emphasized that although the majority of those who made up the congregations might not have enjoyed the benefit of formal education, they were nevertheless intelligent and self-educated. ... Any Welshman can be proud of his forebears from this age - they may have been gnarled by hardship, their hands were usually battered and misshapen as a result of having worked from childhood, they knew nothing of ease or luxury, but they pondered over the higher things of life in their Sunday schools or lamplit homes; they sang hymns with understanding for the words and the music; they spoke their language in all its richness and purity. There is one fact of which Welsh people can be proud, namely, that there was a period when the Principality could claim to have the most cultured working class in the world and the credit for that should go to the chapels and churches'. In 1949 the first Comprehensive Secondary School in England and Wales was opened in Holyhead.

It does not follow that the people were lacking in a sense of humour; there is a similarity between Holyhead and Caernarfon in some respects, the harbour, personalities, (the heavyweights Lewis and William Morris and Robert Roberts the Almanacker in the 18th century), publishing, and witty lawyers in the courts and outside. In *Holyhead the Story of a Port* an anecdote is recalled about a solicitor, T R Evans, whose dog stole a steak from a butcher's shop. When Evans came past the shop the butcher asked him: 'Mr Evans, if a dog were to take meat from my counter what would I be able to do about it?' 'Recover the cost of the meat from the owner' came the reply. 'In that case you owe me five shillings sir.' 'Oh dear. Well, my advice to you comes to six shillings and eight pence. We'll deduct five shillings for the meat, so you owe me one shilling and eight pence'.

'Give him the job and he will finish the tools'. (School Report).

Lewis Morris (1701-65), in addition to his work as a writer, scholar and publisher undertook a very ambitious project the results of which he published under the title '*Plans of Harbours, Bays and Roads in St George's and the Bristol Channel'*. Born at the foot of Mynydd Bodafon he worked and lived in Holyhead as did his brother William who was Collector of Customs, a keen gardener and botanist, a great letter writer and collector of manuscripts. Another brother Richard worked in London and became 'Chief Clerk for Foreign Accounts to the Comptroller of the Navy'. He was very interested in literature and was a collector of manuscripts from an early age. John, the youngest brother died when he was thirty four on board HMS *Torbay* on which he was serving as First Officer.

The rivalry between the Dublin Steam Packet Company and the LNWR was a feature of the port activities around the turn of the century but in 1921 the railway company became the London Midland and Scottish and it secured the mail contract. The withdrawal of the Dublin Steam Packet Company signalled the start of a slump for Holyhead before the general depression of the thirties. The mail and passenger ferries which continued until the Second World War were called: *Anglia, Hibernia, Cambria and Scotia.* In 1949 two new, modern 5,200 ton ships, the *Cambria* and *Hibernia* together with the *Princess Maude* provided the service. The car ferry operating from the Admiralty Pier started in 1965 and another major innovation was the container terminal. The old impressive red brick Station Hotel was closed in 1951 and has since been demolished.

Llanddwyn near Newborough *Photo O Gwyn Jones*

The Breakwater Holyhead

The 'Clio' moored in Straits and 'St Tudno 2' (1891-1912)

In 1801 the population was 2,132; by 1851 it was 8,863. Gas was introduced in 1856 while water was piped from Llyn Traffwll in 1866. At that time the residents would recall the year 1859, the *Royal Charter* shipwreck and the religious revival but for them also, the visit of the transatlantic paddle steamship, the big ship, the *Great Eastern.* In the meantime some of the finest racehorses, the pride of Ireland, have gone through unnoticed. From Bangor and anywhere in Anglesey it takes less than an hour to reach the port.

The Anglesey Aluminium works is just outside Holyhead. The raw material alumina is brought in ships to the company pier and then conveyed by an underground tunnel to be converted into aluminium. The process involves using a large supply of electricity mainly supplied by Wylfa Nuclear Power Station. There are around 600 employees. This industry was brought to Holyhead when Cledwyn Hughes was MP for Anglesey.

There are windows made by William Morris and designed by Burne Jones in the parish church of St Cybi, Holyhead which together with the churchyard and the ancient Capel y Bedd are situated inside the walls of the Roman coast guard fort. In the 6th century the monk Cybi was allowed to settle here probably by Maelgwn the great king of Gwynedd. The oldest part of the present church dates from the 13th century. Another influential ecclesiastic associated with this church and monastery was Elfodd (d. 809), an important bishop in Gwynedd who, though a member of the Welsh church, adopted in 768 AD the Roman method of deciding the date of Easter Sunday. The church is regarded as one of the finest in Gwynedd.

TO THE EMERALD ISLE

The Irish Ferries super ferry *Isle of Inishmore,* launched in March 1997 and which cost £65 million, sails from Holyhead at 3.45am and 3.45pm and takes three and a half hours or less to reach Dublin Port carrying passengers, cars and freight. Very cheap day returns are available, the duty-free mini cruise from only £10 per adult day return or £24 family ticket. It is a great experience to sail in this luxurious ship and to go on the top deck to see the rugged coast and the lighthouses of Anglesey and the Wicklow mountains on the other side. Telephone: Holyhead 0990 134324 - Liverpool 0990 171717.

The other service is the Stena Line. The large ferry ship carrying passengers, cars and freight is the *Challenger* leaving Holyhead at 3.15pm for Dublin Port. There is also the new ship, the world's largest fast ferry known as the HSS (High Speed Sea Service) to Dun Laoghaire crossing in just ninety nine minutes. It is very large and luxurious and can carry 1500 passengers and 375 vehicles. Capable of travelling at 40 knots it claims to give a very smooth crossing while all the facilities on board are really exciting. Day trips are offered for £10 and family ticket £26. Sailing times are; 04.10, 08.55, 13.45, 18.25, 23.05. Telephone: 0990 707070.

BENLLECH BAY

From Llanfair Pwllgwyngyll one can choose to go to the seaside or go fishing at one of the many beaches on the south west coast of the island or the most attractive Cemaes and others on the northern side or the popular and pleasant Benllech Bay sheltered from the south west wind and providing safe bathing on the sandy beach.

About 2 miles (3.2km) inland from Benllech at Bryn Teg is the birth-place of Môn's most famous poet Goronwy Owen (1723-69). Unable to get a curacy in Wales he left for England and eventually secured a post as schoolmaster at William and Mary College, Williamsburg, Virginia. In 1760 he was appointed rector of the parish of St Andrews in the County of Brunswick where he remained for the rest of his life. He was buried in a grove of trees in his own tobacco and cotton plantation. Goronwy was a Latin and Greek scholar whose letters to the Morris brothers mentioned above make fascinating reading. Goronwy Owen, Lewis Morris and their circle by the example of their own compositions and by their discussion of literary criticism had a beneficial influence on many of the poets who followed them.

These literary figures have attracted a great deal of attention over many years in sharp contrast with two men whose roots were in the same neighbourhood, William Jones the mathematician and his son also William Jones. William Jones, senior, (1675-1749) was Vice-President of the Royal Society and was friendly with Newton and Halley. His birthplace, Merddyn was very near that of the Morris brothers at the foot of Mynydd Bodafon. His son Sir William Jones (1746-94) is world-famous as a linguist and an authority on the languages and laws of India.

THE BONESETTERS OF LLANFAIR-YNG-NGHORNWY

Talented in a different field were the famous family of bonesetters starting with Evan Thomas (1735-1814). A boy who spoke Spanish, the sole survivor from a shipwreck off Llanfair-yng-Nghornwy, was adopted by a couple with the surname Thomas. He was the first of a distinguished line of bonesetters and orthopaedic surgeons. Evan Thomas's grandson of the same name became even more famous than his grandfather and moved to Liverpool about 1835. His eldest son Hugh Owen Thomas (1834-91) born at Bodedern, Anglesey, became a very hard working surgeon of outstanding ability. He was so dedicated that he treated working men from the docks in Liverpool without payment. His nephew and pupil was the famous Sir Robert Jones, born in Rhyl in 1857, who during the First World War, used the Thomas Splints and Calipers extensively to very good effect. The memory of his contribution is kept alive in the name of the Robert Jones and Agnes Hunt Orthopaedic Hospital at Gobowen. In 1904, working closely with Agnes Hunt, he changed her Convalescent Home at Baschurch to an orthopaedic hospital in the country supported by clinics in various localities. In 1909 he was appointed the first lecturer in orthopaedic surgery at Liverpool University and in the same year was elected the first president of the orthopaedic department of the International Congress of Medicine.

AMLWCH'S WORLD-FAMOUS COPPER WORKS

In Caernarfonshire the export of slates was responsible for the development of ports and towns at Porthmadog, Caernarfon. Port Dinorwig and Bangor. On Anglesey a similar sequence of events occurred in the case of Amlwch. The extraction of copper by the open cast method, mining and precipitation pits was in itself a vast operation involving about 1,500 workers during the second half of the 18th century. In addition certain subsidiary industries grew; smelting, the production of sulphur and paint and the development of a port to handle imports and the exporting of copper ore. There was a smelting plant belonging to the Parys Mine Company at Greenfield near Holywell. The main imports were coal, iron, building materials including bricks, and domestic requirements. The harbour continued to be improved while on the difficult land around, ship yards with slipways and a dry dock were carved out of the rock. The ship builders were Treweek, Hughes and Thomas, Cox Paynter and William Thomas. Part of the work was maintenance but a large number of ships were built at Amlwch, from a wooden sloop of 7 tons to the *Prince Ja Ja,* a steel steamship of 294 tons. Bryan Hope, in his carefully researched book *A Curious Place,* lists the schooners, sloops and other craft built between 1788 and 1918, forty one made of wood, fourteen of iron and six of steel. The author explains that ship builders generally were at first reluctant to change from wood to iron and began by having the frame of iron retaining wood for cladding before eventually using rolled iron plates for the hull. The phrase 'copper bottomed guarantee' is often used; Hope gives the interesting background to the metaphor. In warm seas the teredo worm, *Teredo Navalis* as long as 3ft (0.9m) and an inch (2.5cm) in diameter, would bore through a ship's planking. By the 1760s it became the practice to sheath hulls with copper plating for protection.

It was during the second half of the 18th century that Amlwch gained prominence because of the copper works which produced as much of the metal as all the other mines in Britain combined. In its day it was the most famous mine in the world, able to control the price of copper on a European scale. The land and the rights belonged to two Anglesey landowners but the one man who made the project such a success was an Anglesey lawyer and land agent, Thomas Williams who lived for some time at Llanidan Hall, Brynsiencyn. He was the son of Owen Williams of Cefn Coch, Llansadwrn and was at one time a solicitor's assistant in Beaumaris. He was primarily a catalyst and a shrewd businessman, evidently well liked since he was called Twm Chwarae Teg (Tom Fair Play) a tribute to his honesty in business and fairness towards his workers. He was also called 'Copper King' because it was in this industry that he showed his great ability. It is a compliment to say that becoming an MP for a constituency in Buckinghamshire was one of his lesser achievements. Thomas Williams died in 1801 and was buried in the graveyard of the old church at Llanidan but was exhumed in 1832 and his remains were buried at Llandegfan the day before his son, Owen Williams MP, of Craig-y-don was buried in the same grave.

Even in Amlwch in the heyday of the port and the copper works life was not entirely hard work; Saturday was a day of rest for the miners, and young boys, on fine Saturday afternoons, would take the farmers' horses into the sea to get rid of the copper dust. And there was locally produced tobacco to chew and smoke. As happened in the large port of Bristol, Amlwch developed a tobacco industry, one firm, E Morgan & Co continuing to supply such brands as 'Baco'r Aelwyd' until the 1940's.

It was known that the copper deposits were worked in Roman times but it has recently been established that there was surface working and mine exploitation during the Bronze Age around 2,000 BC as there was on the Great Orme.

From 1973 to 1987 Shell had a marine oil terminal off Amlwch with a tank farm at Rhosgoch and a pipeline across Anglesey and the Lafan Sands to Stanlow refinery. Tankers of over 500,000 tonnes brought crude oil to this point. Right on the edge of the sea is Octel's Amlwch Works where Bromine is extracted from sea water. This chemical is essential for the production of a large number of products.

Melin Llynnon, Llanddeusant, Anglesey Photo: Ieuan Owen

University College of North Wales Bangor

Normal College Hostels Bangor

The **Cathedral** and the Bishop of Bangor

The monastery with a large number of monks' cells covered a large area. Monks from Bangor Fawr yn Arfon founded the one at Bangor -Is-y- Coed near Wrexham and Bangor, Northern Ireland was probably established on the same pattern.

The Bishop authorised four fairs every year on the Caernarfonshire side of the Porthaethwy Ferry. Later, farmers set up a rival fair at Porthaethwy, **Ffair Borth** which became the biggest in the area. Originally, animals were sold on the streets. During the first part of the 20th Century the horse sale at the Auctioneers yard, where Pioneer supermarket now stands, became a very important event on the 24th of October.

CAERNARFONSHIRE

PENRHYN CASTLE, BANGOR - NATIONAL TRUST PROPERTY

This is a large mansion in the form of a castle built between 1820 and 1845 and a tribute to the high quality workmanship of local stone masons, joiners and carpenters. There are massive oak doors and pieces of furniture and a collection of old masters. Outside there is a most interesting Industrial Railway Museum including locomotives and trucks. The medieval hall at Penrhyn, the home of the family of Gwilym ap Gruffydd who changed his name to Griffith was altered and in the 19th century replaced by the mock 'castle'. A most interesting private house from the 15th century, Cochwillan, built by a younger William ap Gruffydd who fought for Henry VII at Bosworth has been restored and is just over a mile from Penrhyn. His son, taking the father's name as surname, Williams, was able to acquire the former manor of the bishops of Bangor and build the mansion, Y Faenol, there.

THE CITY OF BANGOR

Apart from tourists, over the years many thousands of mainly young people from different countries have made this area their home for a few years as students at the University of Wales, Bangor. The University owns many departmental buildings and hostels the most impressive being the grey sandstone Arts and Libraries edifice on a hill overlooking the town which was completed in 1911, the architect being Henry Hare. For the first years of its life the college occupied the old Penrhyn Arms hotel part of which remains in the form of an arch in a small park on the right going out of Bangor towards Conwy.

Recently incorporated into the University, the teachers' training college, the Normal, was originally in a fine building built of Penmon stone overlooking the Menai Straits. This was built in 1862 the designer being John Barnet of London and the builders W T Rogers of Beaumaris in co-operation with the architect Henry Kennedy who was responsible for the churches St Mary's in Bangor and Menai Bridge, St James' in Upper Bangor and Llandwrog. Barnet based his plan of the Normal College on Montacute House, a Tudor mansion near Yeovil in Somerset now owned by the National Trust. This masterpiece of Tudor architecture was designed by John Thorpe the finest architect of his day for Sir Edward Phelps between 1580 and 1601. The halls of residence nearby were designed by the architect Henry Hare.

Older than the Normal was the Tudor Grammar School, Friars, whose first home, the converted Dominican (Black) friars building was in the Hirael part of Bangor.

Early in the 20th century a new attractive school was built in Upper Bangor and as this was a boys' school, a new County School for girls was built not far away. Friars, no longer for boys only, has moved to Eithinog while Tryfan secondary school concentrates on Welsh-medium education. The Friars building will soon be taken over by Coleg Menai the important expanding tertiary college.

Much older again than Friars is the Cathedral in the centre not very far from the site where Deiniol founded his cell in the 6th century. It is claimed that it is the oldest cathedral but one in Britain. The city is in a valley and higher up from the cathedral is the still busy railway station and higher up still there has recently been constant development so that there are a number of large stores along Caernarfon Road. There is a large District Hospital, Ysbyty Gwynedd on high ground above the town. The BBC has had studios in Bangor for many years and they have made a distinguished contribution to Welsh broadcasting particularly Welsh language programmes and radio. Near the cathedral and the central bus station the art gallery and museum has interesting exhibits. The most important theatre in the area, Theatr Gwynedd is conveniently close by as is the Tourist Information Centre, in the Town Hall, once the Bishop's Palace.

The most attractive part of Bangor is the wooded area around Siliwen and the recently restored pier which seems to reach across almost to Anglesey. A most delightful outing by car or bus is to the village of Abergwyngregyn 7 miles (11km) away, the site of the 13th century palace of the princes of Gwynedd. From the village it is about a 2 mile (3km) walk to the 170ft (51m) waterfall, Rhaeadr fawr.

CAERNARFON

Unlike Beaumaris which for centuries has been mainly English, Caernarfon can rightly claim to be the most distinctly Welsh town in Wales. It can also claim to be its oldest real town, going back nearly two thousand years. According to Nennius in *Historia Brittonum* writing about 800 AD, it was named as one of the three chief cities of Wales; there certainly was a town outside the walls of the military establishment. Julius Agricola was the Roman general who decided to build Segontium (Caer Saint) in 77 AD. The fort covering six acres was rebuilt with stone around 200 AD and held a garrison of 800 men. The Romans decided that this was a strategic site near the entrance to the Menai Straits, with the River Seiont, having its source in Llyn Peris and Llyn Padarn, slightly to the south west. The remains and the small museum describing the fort and the Romans, who left finally in 385 AD, are well worth a visit. The Roman road from Caersaint to Caerhun in the Conwy Valley kept on the high ground to Dinas Dinorwig and slightly inland from Bangor to Aber. Milestones which have been discovered on this route may be seen at the Bangor Museum.

A notable feature of Caernarfon is the open space at the centre, near the castle, called in Welsh 'Y Maes'; there is one in Pwllheli as well. It dates from 1817 when a hillock that had been used as a place for cock fighting was removed as a measure to relieve unemployment. After 1800, houses began to be built outside the town walls and as a result of the Municipal Corporations Act 1835 further improvements were made to the town. A water supply system from Llyn Cwellyn had been installed in 1829. The new prison, which later was adapted to become the headquarters of the Caernarfonshire and later still in 1973, Gwynedd County Council, was built in 1867. The paved path around the town walls with views across the sea towards Anglesey provide a memorable walk especially at sunset.

There are two statues in Castle Square, one bronze of David Lloyd George (1863-1945) by William Goscombe John and another bronze of Sir Hugh Owen (1804-1881) by J Milo Griffith. Hugh Owen was the prime mover in founding the University College of Wales, Aberystwyth (1872) and with John Phillips the Normal College, Bangor. For these achievements and his tireless work in promoting elementary education he deserves to be remembered on the same square as Lloyd George. It is also fitting that his memorial stands in Caernarfon for it was the market town for Dwyran, Newborough and Brynsiencyn where he grew up and he attended school in the town.

PLAS MENAI NATIONAL WATERSPORTS CENTRE

There are plenty of opportunities for exhilarating watersports in the area. Plas Menai on the Menai Straits or Llanfair-is-gaer near Caernarfon has facilities for windsurfing, sailing, rowing, canoeing and multiactivity courses including mountain sports. Telephone: 01248 670964.

CAERNARFON AIR WORLD

An unusual and very exciting way of seeing Caernarfon castle, one of the finest in existence, with its pentagonal, octagonal and hexagonal towers and very widely known because of the television coverage of the investiture of the Prince of Wales in 1969, is to take a pleasure flight from *Caernarfon Air World* by Dinas Dinlle 7 miles (11km) from Caernarfon. Flights are available also over Bardsey Island, Tremadog Bay, Snowdon, (a breathtaking twenty minute experience) and along the Straits to Beaumaris and back. Originally built as RAF Llandwrog aerodrome, the first RAF Mountain Rescue team was formed there, a service, now from RAF Valley, that has been invaluable over the years together with the dedication of the volunteers of the Llanberis Mountain Rescue Team. There is also an air museum open from 1 March to 2 November and a coffee shop and restaurant, refreshments being available every day as are the flights, weather permitting.

There is no known connection between the great architect and the Inigo Jones Slateworks at **Groeslon** near Caernarfon where the public can see craftsmen cutting, shaping and polishing slate slabs. It has been voted the best craft workshop in Wales.

SMALL SHIPS SMALL PORTS

As Holyhead and Menai Bridge were developing Beaumaris had been in steady decline as a port while Caernarfon, in 1844 was able to free itself from the shackles of the old customs port. During the middle years of the 19th century the ships carrying emigrants to America were bringing back wheat and timber to Caernarfon. Until the introduction of steamships around 1850 the small ports such as Amlwch, Traeth Coch, Cemaes and Porthaethwy in Anglesey and Porthdinllaen, Pwllheli, Nefyn and Conwy in Caernarfonshire were very busy dealing with the brigs, sloops and schooners importing coal, iron, timber, salt, rice and various other goods as well as the harvest of the sea. Because the railway station at Pwllheli was a fair distance away the old fashion continued at Porth Colmon; earthenware pots, guano, flour and animal foodstuffs were brought in by sea and coal ships used to come until the 1920's. In the same way as the area around Beaumaris was about 8 miles (13km) from Llanfair station, coal was brought by ship to Fryars Bay as late as the 1930's. Some of the coal brought into the small ports was used with local or imported limestone to produce lime for building and as a fertilizer in many small lime kilns. The small ships were doing work taken over later by the railway freight trucks and today largely by lorries while the ports acted like the garages of today not only repairing but also building wooden ships. The main ship-building, centres were Pwllheli, Porthmadog, Holyhead and Amlwch. During the first half of the 20th century the marine engineering section of the port was a most important part of the harbour complex at Holyhead.

A PENINSULA AND AN ISLAND

From the earliest part of the first millennium invasion and colonization by the **Irish** was a constant threat on the western shores of Wales. The Romans built a fort near the sea at Holyhead around 300 AD and it is claimed that Brythonic reinforcements from what is now the north of England and southern Scotland. came to defend Gwynedd during the 5th century. The leader of this expedition was Cunedda who probably consolidated his position on both sides of the Menai Straits from where his descendants were able to regain more extensive territories. Cunedda, the soldier king from a heavily Romanized family in Northern Britain was the founder of the Gwynedd royal line including Rhodri Mawr, Hywel Dda and Gruffudd ap Cynan. Part of the evidence for the continued presence of the Irish remains in the place-names Llŷn with its alternative spelling, Lleyn, and Porth

Dinllaen. Some everyday Welsh words are derived from Irish e.g. brechdan (butty) < *brechtan;* brat (apron) < *brat*; and cerbyd (vehicle) < *carpat.* The ogham inscriptions on ancient stones point in the same direction.

There were Iron Age hill-forts near the coast at Dinllaen in Llŷn and Dinas Dinlle in Arfon and many inland such as Castell Odo, Garn Fadrun and Garn Boduan, fairly close to each other in Llŷn.

DAVID LLOYD GEORGE

According to the tribal divisions **Llŷn** was a *cantref* (literally a hundred communities) at the tip of the peninsula with its boundary running from the south coast near Afon Wen to the north near Trefor. Yr Eifl consisting of three peaks reaching 1,849ft (563m), and Garn Fadryn at 1,217ft (370m) are considerably higher than the highest point on Anglesey, Mynydd Twr, Holyhead at 720ft (219m). The area around Criccieth is the commote of **Eifionydd**. Here near the River Dwyfor is the birth-place and grave of David Lloyd George 'the cottage bred boy who became Prime Minister' as the brochure says. He has been remembered with gratitude for many years for the Old Age Pension Act. In 1916 he became the United Kingdom's first Welsh Prime Minister. As a prominent MP he lived at Bryn Awelon, Criccieth but he spent his childhood at Llanystumdwy. His grave is near his first home beside the River Dwyfor; he did not wish to be buried in Westminster Abbey. He said to his brother William: 'That is where I want to be buried. That is the stone which I sit on to admire the view of the river. I want no inscription on my grave, only that boulder'. The memorial museum and the grave enclosure, consisting of a curved stone wall and wrought iron work, were designed by the renowned architect, Clough Williams Ellis, the creator of Portmeirion.

When he was Chancellor of the Exchequer there was a dramatic conflict between the Liberals and the House of Lords over the great budget of 1909. Lloyd George revelled in the fight involving important issues that divided Liberalism from Toryism; he was making a stand on behalf of the poor and deprived. With the oppression of landlordism fresh in his memory he was leading in the class struggle and sympathetic to the grievances of workers in industrial areas before Labour became a force. He made brilliant speeches such as that at Newcastle when he said, as reported for example by J Hugh Edwards in his *Life of Lloyd George*: 'Questions will be asked which are now whispered in humble voices, and answers will be demanded then with authority. The question will be whether five hundred men, ordinary men chosen accidentally from among the unemployed, shall override the judgement of millions of people who are engaged in the industry which makes the wealth of the country. That is one question. Another will be, who ordained that a few should have the land of Britain as a perquisite? Who made ten thousand people owners of the soil and the rest of us trespassers in the land of our birth?' His peroration in a speech on his home ground, Caernarfon, is being talked about to this day. 'Yesterday, I visited the old village where I was brought up. I wandered through the woods familiar to my boyhood. There I saw a child getting sticks for firewood, and I thought of the hours which I spent in the same pleasant and profitable occupation, for I have been something of a backwoodsman; and here is one experience taught me then which is of use to me today. I learnt as a child it was little use going into the woods after a period of calm and fine weather, for I generally returned empty handed. But after a great storm I always came back with an armful. We are in for rough weather; we may be even in for a winter of storms which will rock the forest, break many a withered branch, and leave many a rotten tree torn up by the roots, but when the weather clears you may depend upon it there will be something brought within reach of the people that will give warmth and glow to their grey lives, something that will help to dispel the hunger, the despair, the oppression and the wrong which now chill so many of their hearths'.

John Hugh Edwards in his *Life of Lloyd George* quotes from a speech by Lloyd George in the House of Commons: 'You cannot go into a peasant's house or into a shepherd's cottage without hearing the names of the great Non-Conformist preachers who made Wales what it is today'. The same author records that the place of honour in the dining room of his official residence in Downing Street was occupied by a portrait of the great preacher, former quarryman, John Jones Talysarn.

His oratory however was not the only reason for his success. With his clear vision and careful planning, his steadfastness of purpose and his tenacity he was able to get things done, great things.

BARDSEY ISLAND

In medieval times it is possible that some of the pilgrims on their way to Ynys Enlli from Beddgelert would come through Llanystumdwy and Abererch while many would travel by sea near the coast calling at some of the churches situated close to the shore. However the main route seems to have been near the northern coast through Clynnog with a resting station at Llanaelhaearn. The parish church of St Beuno at Clynnog Fawr is a large, fine building dating almost entirely from 1,500 AD on the site of Beuno's original chapel near an important monastery of the 7th century. The saint's tomb and the well, Ffynnon Beuno were places of pilgrimage and it was the custom to bring the sick to them as late as the 18th century. There was a fairly good road called the Pilgrims' Way to Aberdaron and the sheltered Porth Meudwy, the usual embarking point for Bardsey. As the pilgrims travelled long distances it was pre-arranged that monasteries should provide lodging and sustenance for them.

Nant Gwrtheyrn, below Llithfaen, formerly a deserted quarrying village, and subsequently a Welsh Language Centre, according to tradition was associated with a High King of Britain, Vortigern. Threatened by the Picts from the North he employed the other invaders, the Saxons to help him and had to yield territory to them in payment. He is associated with Dinas Emrys, Beddgelert, where he was deposed by a rival, Emrys or *Ambrosius*. Utterly condemned and rejected by fellow Brythons for the great betrayal, he had to retire to this very remote valley to die. After Llanaelhaearn there was a resting place for pilgrims to Bardsey at Pistyll church near Nefyn. The grave of the actor Rupert Davies who became well known as the detective Maigret in the television series is in this churchyard.

The most attractive church in Llŷn today, Llangwnnadl, during the Middle Ages provided another hospice for pilgrims while in Aberdaron they could refresh themselves finally at Y Gegin Fawr (The Large Kitchen) before venturing on the dangerous crossing. The area of the island which is roughly 2 miles (3.2km) in length is about 450 acres. It was a sacred place of retreat where a large number of Christian missionaries, monks or saints, it is claimed, were buried. Three pilgrimages to Enlli were equivalent to one to Rome. Fishing has traditionally been the main employment and there was a thriving farming community until 1926 when many residents left including the last 'king' or elected arbitrator whose name was Love Pritchard. The automatic lighthouse is still important and a small number of people live on the island including the personnel who man the bird observation station. Access is through personal contact with competent and reliable local boatmen from Aberdaron.

PLAS YN RHIW

One delightful place to visit, four miles to the east from Aberdaron is Plas yn Rhiw, now a National Trust property. Three sisters Eileen, Honora and Lorna Keatings in 1939 were able to acquire the neglected house and small estate and spent many years restoring the house and garden. It was not a stately home but a large farmhouse of character from the 17th century. Stone-built with evenly spaced sash windows and an overhanging roof it is a good example of how an old house should be restored. It is situated on a wooded slope above Porth Neigwl. The sisters donated Plas yn Rhiw to the National Trust in 1949 in honour of their parents.

There were, in Llŷn as in other parts of Wales earlier mansions where the land-owning aristocracy enjoyed good food and wine and continued as the traditional patrons of poets and musicians. Wiliam Llŷn (1534-1580) who was from this area lived towards the end of the period of patronage. He was a teacher of poets and is the author of an excellent elegy to his own teacher Gruffydd Hiraethog.

PWLLHELI

Pwllheli and Nefyn became boroughs in 1355, Nefyn concentrating on fishing and Pwllheli becoming an important port for sailing ships. Many wooden ships were built at both ports and at Porthmadog, Porthdinllaen, Y Felinheli, Bangor and Conwy. Pwllheli on the South coast of the Llŷn peninsula is central and has always been the market town for the rural area. Hardly any of the sailors, including the Duke of Edinburgh, who were stationed at the camp HMS Glendower on Penychain Farm land and called the place *Penny Chain,* or the visitors who stayed at Butlin's Holiday Camp, later Starcoast World, would know anything about Pwllheli's most famous poet of the 20th century, Cynan (A E Jones) who made his name with his poems of the First World War and later as the colourful archdruid of the Gorsedd at the National Eisteddfod. Cynan lived in Porthaethwy for many years and was buried at St Tysilio where are also the graves of the Rev Henry Rees and the eminent Welsh historian Sir J E Lloyd. Nor would they know about Y Lôn Goed, the green lane with an avenue of trees immortalized in a poem by R Williams Parry one of the outstanding poets of the 20th century. Even without knowing the literary association one can enjoy a peaceful walk along this lane north from the Afon Wen estuary. It was made for the convenience of the local farms in 1817 by an Englishman John Maughan.

Not far away was the place where the three Welsh Nationalists, Saunders Lewis, L E Valentine and D J Williams in September 1936 set fire to the temporary buildings in preparation for the RAF bombing training school at Penyberth. The so-called 'extremists' prepared thoroughly for the conflagration, spraying petrol liberally over the timber, and when the fire was well under way they went to Pwllheli police station to report the incident and face the consequences. The jury at Caernarfon Assizes could not agree on a verdict and there was bitter disappointment when the case was transferred to the Old Bailey in London. They spent nine months in Wormwood Scrubs having kindled a new patriotism in the hearts of many Welsh people. Perhaps the dramatic confrontation was inevitable in view of the widespread opposition to the proposals and the arrogant refusal of the Government to listen, but it is debatable whether it was the right move for a twelve year old democratic political party to make. The National Party of Wales was established in a small way in a cafe, later Siop Ensor, in Pwllheli in 1925. The badge of the party consisting of three pointed triangles based on the view of the peaks of Snowdonia from Llanfair Pwllgwyngyll, was designed by Richard Llywelyn Hughes at a house called Coedlys. It took Plaid Cymru until 1966 to win its first parliamentary seat when

Gwynfor Evans was successful after the death of Lady Megan Lloyd George who had been the Liberal MP for Anglesey for many years and was thereafter the Labour member for Carmarthen. Megan was the first woman MP to be elected in Wales. But the Second World War was a major factor that hindered the development of the new party and it could be argued that nothing short of direct action could have shaken the nation out of its torpor in 1936. Direct action as a political tool eventually led, through Saunders Lewis's radio lecture in 1962, to the vigorous and determined campaigns of *Cymdeithas yr Iaith,* the Welsh Language Society. It is significant that three of the four seats held by Plaid Cymru are in this area of North West Wales.

CLEAN BEACHES

The Green Sea Partnership in which Dŵr Cymru (Welsh Water) co-operating with local authorities, private companies, Government and voluntary organisations is well ahead with its clean coastline plan.

By 1998 a total of fifteen Welsh beaches had been awarded the Blue Flag for excellence, seven of them in North Wales. The Blue Flag is awarded annually to those beaches meeting a total of twenty six stringent criteria covering bathing water quality and safety, services, facilities and environmental education. In the area covered in this book the following six beaches have won the Blue Flag: Llanddona, Llanddwyn, Abersoch, Abermaw, Dinas Dinlle and Pwllheli.

Pwllheli marina one of the finest in North Wales, won a Marina Blue Flag in 1998. **It is well to remember that the sea can be very dangerous. It is vitally important for those wishing to enjoy the beaches and the sea to have proper equipment, to take adequate precautions and to think of others.**

Sailing on Straits *Photo Ieuan Owen*

Gwynedd County Council Headquarters

Glynllifon Workshops

Gwynedd County Council

EPILOGUE

GWYNEDD COUNTY COUNCIL (1974-1996)

For twenty-two years there was one County Council for the area covered in this book. This regional council was mainly composed of Anglesey, Caernarfonshire and Meirionnydd, three counties which were established by Edward I in 1284, together with a small portion of Denbighshire around Llanrwst. More significant was the fact that it included most of the old Principality of Llywelyn the Great and Llywelyn the Last. Over sixty per cent of the county was either in the Snowdonia National Park or in designated Areas of Outstanding Natural Beauty. Snowdonia, spreading over 2,175 square kilometres (840 square miles), is, next to the Lake District, the largest of Britain's National Parks. It extends from the Dyfi estuary in the south to Conwy in the north. Most of the coastline of Anglesey and the Llŷn Peninsula are Areas of Outstanding Natural Beauty, and there are ninety miles of Heritage Coast. Welsh is used for much of the county's commerce and administration and it is used by local people in all aspects of their lives. Gwynedd County Council's committees and publications were all bilingual.

WILDLIFE

In a short piece about **wildlife** in Gwynedd William Condry wrote: 'South of Snowdon the mountains continue all the way to the Dyfi estuary. The Rhinog range near Barmouth, Arennig near Bala, Aran Fawddwy in the south-east and Cader Idris near Dolgellau; all these mountains have their individuality; all are rewarding for their fauna and flora. ... The noble white limestone headland, the Great Orme at Llandudno, has long been known for its wild flowers, its seabirds and its butterflies ... South Stack's wild flowers are many, and no matter where you go along the coast of Anglesey, north or south, the natural rock gardens of the cliff slopes go with you for many miles. In the east of Anglesey you reach cliffs that are white with limestone. Here are many wild flowers not known in limeless districts; and a little inland are marshes and fens preserved for their rare sedges, orchids and other treasures'.

Professor Tom Pritchard, in the same vein wrote: 'Edward Lhuyd, one of Wales's most gifted scholars had come across another bequest of the ice fields - the Snowdon lily, a small, beautiful plant, Lili'r Wyddfa in Welsh, *Lloydia serotina* in scientific Latin. The inaccessible crags above Llyn Idwal have uninterruptedly served as the habitat of this plant, the rarest of the Welsh arctic-alpine flora. Generations of naturalists have studied the mountains of Gwynedd since Edward Lhuyd's explorations. They too discovered many new things - the uniqueness of the place, the biological wealth and variety in the landscape, the scientific importance of its natural environment. No wonder that Wales's first National Nature Reserve was established in Cwm Idwal. ... Nature to this day is a powerful force in this county, and the mountains remain a green fortress. Gwynedd's natural environment survived the upheavals of generations of pastoralists and farmers, of some woodmen and of copper and lead miners, quarrymen and seamen; and tourists from the Victorian age onwards. The landscape did not lose its personality; it changed, and in some ways was diversified by the combination of human activities and natural forces'.

SENSITIVE DEVELOPMENT

Iorwerth Roberts of the Daily Post, wrote: 'Though it has been a tourist destination for well over a century, Gwynedd is fortunate that its potential has not been spoilt by over-exploitation. The chances are that with the care that is now being taken in developing that potential, this north-west corner of Wales will avoid the excesses which have made other parts of the British Isles over-commercialized and have cheapened their image'.

The County Council produced an environmental strategy committing itself to attempting to avoid the use of environmentally damaging materials and practices, and Gwynedd was the first local authority in Wales to produce a comprehensive report on the health of its environment. Public transport is more environmentally acceptable than the car and Gwynedd County Council's public transport system, marketed under the Welsh brand name 'Bws Gwynedd' was acknowledged as one of the best rural public transport networks in Britain. When Gwynedd County Council was created services were in decline. Parts of the rail network had closed together with a number of the smaller stations, and bus services had been reduced. Gwynedd's positive policies reversed this decline and began the process of building up the healthy and vigorous system which still exists. Gwynedd was one of the first counties to produce a bus map and timetables starting in 1979. 'Clipa' minibus routes were introduced from 1986 providing more frequent services and serving areas previously inaccessible for buses. Around the mountains of northern Snowdonia 'the Sherpa' buses are a familiar sight and are an asset to the walker and the carless.

The County Council was well aware of the importance of conservation but protected lands have to be managed and enhanced with great sensitivity so as to allow for industrial, tourist and other enterprises which are essential to the economic and social well-being of the county. Iorwerth Roberts put it this way: 'For most people beaches, mountains and castles are the primary reasons for coming to Gwynedd, but there is more, far more to the region than that. The involvement of Gwynedd County Council in this all-important sector of the local economy has been growing, taking advantage of opportunities as they occur, and in effect filling in some of the gaps that private tourist operators may not be in a position to exploit. The workshops at the old manor house, Glynllifon, have been restored with every attempt being made to retain the original atmosphere of industrial workshops in a rural setting. The old single cylinder steam engine dating back to 1854 has been brought back to life, its tall chimney restored by steeplejack and steam enthusiast Fred Dibnah. Centrepiece of the park is the tourist centre with craftsmen and artists renting workshop or studio space. ... Lovely walks through well-kept gardens are enhanced by the allocation of areas to specific themes. Drama, children's literature and the writers of Gwynedd are some of the themes depicted'. Not too far away is Parc Padarn at Llanberis with the quarrying museum. Strong links with local schools have been forged at both parks. Tŷ Meirion, an architecturally pleasing building in the centre of Dolgellau, celebrates the history of the Quakers in that area of Gwynedd.

ARCHITECTURE

The restored workshops at Parc Glynllifon are a lasting tribute to the County Architect's Department and there are other numerous examples of fine buildings, such as the new primary school at Penisarwaun. They were responsible for the exciting new Snowdonia National Park offices with an innovative and conservation conscious design at Penrhyndeudraeth. The most important accolade they received was for the new County Council headquarters itself in Caernarfon. Residents and visitors alike have taken to the building and so have architectural experts. Pencadlys Gwynedd was awarded a major Civic Trust Award in 1986 and also the Gold Medal Award for Architecture of the National Eisteddfod of Wales. The Design Consultant, Professor Dewi Prys Thomas, explaining that continental influences had been at work said: 'Essentially the Pencadlys tries as a major public building, while singing in harmony with the great castle alongside, not to overwhelm the small houses of the town by its size and scale, their colour, their slate roofs. It is, in fact, a very Welsh building'.

REGIONAL PLANNING

The area of the regional county, stretching from Aberdaron to Llandudno and from Amlwch and Holyhead to Aberdyfi and Bala, was large. In terms of economic development and strategic planning, highways and transportation, further education, culture and leisure, as well as general and financial administration, economies of scale were possible. Although the land covered was extensive the population was only about 250,000. The council ensured that as little as possible of its budget was spent on administrative overheads. Of Gwynedd County Council's staff eighty-five per cent worked 'at the sharp end', in schools, in libraries, in homes for the elderly, on the roads and in many other areas of community life. The Fire Service under the Public Protection Committee was a County Council responsibility. During the Aberconwy floods of 1993, almost a thousand calls were received and, at the height of the flooding, twenty-seven water pumps were in use. Much of the emphasis of the Fire Service's work was on fire prevention.

The work of the Trading Standards Department had become extremely complicated because of modern trends, UK and European Union legislation. In 1215 AD matters were simpler; Magna Carta pronounced: 'There shall be one measure of ale throughout the land'.

After 1988 central government policy made it necessary to establish three trading units operating as 'arm's length' companies under the overall control of the Council. They were Gwynedd Civil Engineering, Gwynedd Training and Gwynedd Commercial Services.

ECONOMIC DEVELOPMENT

The Economic Development Department was able to attract Welsh Office and European grants for many and varied projects. An effective telecommunication network has been put in place, including the establishment of six Telecentres. The Council has supported many pioneering projects in the county, including the Snowdonia Bic (Business Innovation Centre). The Department set up small workshops, where individuals can start up on their own or by employing two or three. One significant innovation is MENTEC in Bangor, a technology centre on the university campus where high-tech companies can become established. A European Unit was set up at the beginning of the nineties, which has attracted finance from several European funds. As well as securing annual grants from the European Regional Development Fund and the European Social Fund towards projects designated to strengthen the county's economy and improve the quality of life, Gwynedd secured finance for some of the main European Union programmes, LEADER and INTERREG. The council was alive to the county's strengths and built on them. The most notable example of this has been the practical support given to the growth of the media industry in Gwynedd, following the establishment of the Welsh television channel S4C in 1982. In 1990, with the firm support of the County Council in the form of a loan, BARCUD opened a large television studio in Caernarfon. In 1992 the post of Media Development Officer was created. The dual purpose of the post was to promote the indigenous industry in all its aspects and to market the county as a location for film makers. In 1994 a Hollywood block buster *First Knight* about the Brythonic King Arthur, who lived around 500 AD, was filmed at several locations in the county. A year later, the

Coliseum Cinema, Porthmadog was chosen as the location of the film's European premiere.

Welsh is the language of the majority in North West Wales. The old Gwynedd County Council was co-operating with other European countries having minority languages and working towards a Europe less as a group of large states and more as a family of regions. At the same time, young people, already well grounded in traditional songs and music, were experimenting and extending the boundaries in folk and country songs and through pop and rock groups. And not only were they performing; they set up studios such as those of SAIN near Caernarfon showing modern entrepreneurial skills. Through live performances and records they also were building cultural bridges.

Iorwerth Roberts, at the end of the larger Gwynedd's term of office, recalled the beginning: 'It had all sorts of problems too, not least of which at that stage was rural depopulation. Departing families left vacant properties, some doomed to dereliction, and in the height of the second home boom, these were picked up cheaply as holiday homes, sending prices out of reach of local couples in search of homes. Local employment opportunities were scarce and the level of pay was below the national average'.

Hard economic problems had, therefore, to be faced by the new Council. But the stewardship that was entrusted to Gwynedd County Council was greater than material prosperity - there was a rich linguistic and cultural legacy to be safeguarded and strengthened.

BILINGUAL POLICY

Iorwerth Roberts again: 'One of the most influential decisions of all was the introduction of a bilingual policy in administration. It is difficult after twenty two years of bilingual administration to realize how pioneering that decision was. Simultaneous translation services had been available for full council meetings in Anglesey and Caernarfonshire, but Gwynedd's decision meant documents were produced bilingually, and every committee and sub-committee had an interpreter present to translate simultaneously for the benefit of those who did not understand Welsh. In practice, it meant that every councillor and officer could address meetings in the language of his or her choice. It soon became a predominantly Welsh chamber.

The quality of debate was high, rich in idiomatic Welsh, even when discussing highly technical, fiscal or planning policies. The importance of that bilingual policy cannot be stressed too much, for it influenced the thinking of the Council in many, many ways. For the first time, decisions about the future of *Y Fro Gymraeg* were taken by people in their own language, and subtly, almost imperceptibly, the Council as a whole started to look at its problems from a Welsh point of view.

By recruiting staff able to deliver services to the public in both Welsh and English, Gwynedd County Council was twenty years ahead of the requirements of the Welsh Language Act. When key staff with both professional and linguistic qualifications were unavailable, the Council either provided the means for non-Welsh speaking recruits to learn Welsh to a sufficient level of fluency for their employment or recruited Welsh speaking young people for graduate traineeships in vocations where there were a dearth of bilingual candidates. Thus the citizens of Gwynedd could receive most services in the majority of areas in either language.

Even more crucial was the introduction of a bilingual education policy. It ensured that every child in a school financed by Gwynedd County Council, from ages four to eleven in primary and from twelve to sixteen in secondary education not only studied Welsh as a subject, but also followed subjects through the medium of Welsh as far as their linguistic knowledge permitted. As a pioneer in this particular field, Gwynedd anticipated the 'National Curriculum' by twenty years. A network of immersion centres, for older primary school pupils who arrived in Gwynedd unable to speak Welsh, together with supportive 'Athrawon Bro' (peripatetic teachers), enabled all children to integrate successfully into a predominantly Welsh medium primary school environment. In secondary schools the idea of a 'core curriculum' of Welsh, English, another modern European language, mathematics and science was pioneered. Throughout the period of the Council, education standards remained high, as seen in the county's examination results, which had been consistently higher than the Welsh average.

The Council proved steadfast in its dealings, making the old motto ***CADERNID GWYNEDD*** come true'.

THE SNOWDONIA NATIONAL PARK

Telephone: 01766 770274
The Snowdonia National Park was designated in 1951. For the twenty-two years of the life of the old Gwynedd County Council the Park was administered by a county committee. Concern for residents within the National Park, as well as for visitors has been a common theme during this period. By 1996 the Agricultural Liaison Service had negotiated access agreements over 3,000 hectares of land on Snowdon. It had negotiated over 200 agreements with farmers for the conservation of broad-leaved woodland, valuable wetland and heath and moorland areas as well as reinstatement of many kilometres of dry stone walls and hedgerows and the safeguarding of valuable landscape features such as traditional farm buildings.

The wardens are the eyes and ears of the National Park and effectively represent it to both visiting and local people alike. The local communities within the National Park form a vital part of the intimate fabric of its make-up. The National Park Study Centre at Plas Tan y Bwlch has earned a high reputation for training.

There are tourist information centres at the following places in Snowdonia National Park. Aberdyfi Tel: 01654 767321; Betws-y coed Tel: 01690 710426; Blaenau Ffestiniog Tel: 01766 830360; Dolgellau Tel: 01341 422888; Harlech Tel: 01766 780658. Wardens are available on the following telephone numbers: Pen-y-pas 01286 872555; Nant Peris 01286 870399; Ogwen 01286 602080; Dolgellau 01341 422878 and Llyn Tegid, Y Bala 01678 520626.

Slate splitting Cwt-y-Bugail Blaenau Ffestiniog *Photo Colin Jones*

Gwynedd County Council

The workers have nothing to lose but their chains. They have a world to gain. Workers of the world unite. Karl Marx (1818-1883)

THE LONG, LONG NAME

LLANFAIRPWLLGWYNGYLLGOGERYCHWYRNDROBWLL
LLANDYSILIOGOGOGOGOCH

YOU CAN LEARN HOW TO PRONOUNCE IT
Llan fair pwll gwyn gyll I go ger y chwyrn dro bwll I llan dysilio gogo goch
(English equivalent sounds given)

1. Llan **ll** tongue against top front teeth; let sound out of side of mouth
   an as in ***man***
   fair **f** as *v*; ***ai*** as **eye**; **r** rolled as Scottish Bur(r)ns; so ***veyerr***
   pwll **p** no problem; **w** short as in_***book*; ll** as above
   gwyn as personal name ***Gwyn***
   gyll **g** as in ***Gwyn***; **y** as ***win***; **ll** as above

Now have a rest and go over it a few times.

2. *go as* ***go***
   ger as ***get (gerr)***
   y ***uh*** as in ***up***
   chwyrn **ch** from throat as Scottish ‘loch’
   wy as ***Gwyn*** above
   r rolled
   n no problem
   dro **d** no problem; **r** rolled; **o** as ***song***
   bwll as **pwll** but **b** (no problem)

Have a rest and go over it a few times.

3. llan as above
   dysilio **d** no problem; **y** ***uh***; **s** no problem; **i** as in ***in***; **l** no problem;
   i as above;**o** short as ***song***
   gogo **g** as ***Gwyn***; two short o’s as ***long long***
   goch **g** as above; **o** long as ***go***; **ch** as before

GOGOGOCH!!! CRACKED IT.

Now write it out in three sections and go back to it occasionally. You will now have your party piece ready. Congratulations.

GUIDE TO SELECTED ITEMS

ONE HUNDRED YEARS AGO

1898 The first British Club devoted to rock-climbing, the Climbers' Club, was founded in North Wales.

1898 The first motor buses in Wales came into service at Llandudno.

1898 The steamer *Benholm* sank off Point Lynas, Anglesey drowning ten of the crew.

From *Reference Wales* by John May University of Wales Press

ACTORS IN DIFFERENT FIELDS

Hugh Griffith (1912-1980) of Marian Glas Anglesey.
Awarded an Oscar for his prominent part in the film *Ben Hur.*
Also took part in the films *Tom Jones* and *Run for your Money.*

Sir Ellis Jones Griffith (1860-1926) of Brynsiencyn Anglesey.
First Class Law Tripos at Downing College Cambridge (1883).
Fellow of Downing College (1888) KC (1912).
Elected Liberal MP for Anglesey (1895) with a majority of 1,027
At that time the Parliamentary session did not start in the autumn.

BACK COVER CREDITS

Gwynedd County Council
Anglesey Agricultural Society

1990's Big Spender *Buy now pale later*!